ENGAGED INSTRUCTION

THRIVING CLASSROOMS IN THE AGE OF THE COMMON CORE

ENGAGED INSTRUCTION

THRIVING CLASSROOMS IN THE AGE OF THE COMMON CORE

Tom Hierck
Rachel Syrja
John Almarode
Angela Peery
Lisa Cebelak
Lori Cook
Lynn Howard
Lissa Pijanowski
Ainsley Rose
Gabriel Rshaid
Stephen Ventura
David Nagel
Sharon Delesbore

LEAD+
LEARN
PRESS

ENGLEWOOD, COLORADO

The Leadership and Learning Center
317 Inverness Way South, Suite 150
Englewood, Colorado 80112
Phone 1.866.399.6019 | Fax 303.504.9417
www.leadandlearn.com

Published by Lead + Learn Press, a division of Houghton Mifflin Harcourt.

Library of Congress Cataloging-in-Publication Data

Hierck, Tom.
  Engaged instruction : thriving classrooms in the age of the common core /
Tom Hierck [and 12 others].
    pages cm
  Includes bibliographical references and index.
  ISBN 978-1-935588-48-1 (alk. paper)
  1. Teaching—United States. 2. Education—Standards—United States.
I. Title.
  LB1025.3.H535 2013
  371.102—dc23
                                                              2013031614

ISBN 978-1-935588-48-1

Printed in the United States of America

17 16 15 14 13   01 02 03 04 05 06 07

Contents

About the Authors

Thomas Hierck is a Professional Development Associate with The Leadership and Learning Center. He has been an educator since 1983 in a career that has spanned all grade levels and many roles, including teacher, administrator, district leader, department of education project leader, and executive director. Tom is a coauthor of *Pyramid of Behavior Interventions: Seven Keys to a Positive Learning Environment* (2011), which examines the inextricable link between behavior and academics. He has also contributed chapters to *The Teacher as Assessment Leader* (2009) and *The Principal as Assessment Leader* (2009), and published two books that celebrate the role of the teacher, *What Do You Make?* and *I Am the Future.* Tom's belief that "every student is a success story waiting to be told" has led him to work with teachers and administrators to create positive school cultures and build effective relationships that facilitate learning for all students.

Rachel Carrillo Syrja is a Professional Development Associate with The Leadership and Learning Center. During her 19 years in education, she has been a classroom teacher, mathematics coach and resource teacher, and professional developer. Among her many leadership roles, she has designed and implemented district-wide staff development in the areas of English language development, working with struggling learners, standards-based education, and assessment for learning. Additionally, Rachel has conducted workshops for teachers and administrators on Data Teams, professional learning communities, and using assessment data to drive instruction. She is the author of *How to Reach and Teach English Language Learners* (2011) and *Common Formative Assessments for English Language Learners* (2012). Raised in a bilingual household, Rachel has an acute sense of the needs of English language learners. While working in a district that had a large population of English learners and Title I students, Rachel worked on implementing a stronger program for ELLs district-wide by synthesizing state data and district data to build a comprehensive program that addressed the needs of ELLs at their individual language development levels.

John Almarode is a Professional Development Associate with The Leadership and Learning Center. John began his career in Augusta County, Virginia, teaching secondary mathematics and science to a wide range of students. John has conducted staff development workshops, keynote addresses, and conference presentations on a variety of topics, including student engagement, evidence-based practices, creating enriched environments that promote learning, and designing classrooms with the brain in mind. He has authored multiple publications on these topics and has recently published a book on engaging the student brain in science and mathematics. In addition to his work with The Leadership and Learning Center, John is on the faculty at James Madison University in the College of Education. John, his wife Dani, and their daughter Tessa live in Waynesboro, Virginia.

Angela B. Peery is a Senior Professional Development Associate with The Leadership and Learning Center. Before joining The Center, she was a Teacher Specialist with the South Carolina Department of Education and worked with a chronically low-performing middle school as part of a turnaround team. Angela was also previously a consultant for the National Urban Alliance for Effective Education, co-teaching and designing lessons with teachers in high-poverty, at-risk schools in Seattle and Indianapolis. Angela's experience includes ten years of classroom teaching, four years as a high school assistant principal, and various leadership roles at the building, district, and state levels. She has taught at both the undergraduate and graduate levels for Coastal Carolina University, Horry-Georgetown Technical College, the University of Phoenix, and Kaplan University Online. She was also a codirector of a National Writing Project site for several years. Angela has published six books, including *Writing Matters in Every Classroom*, and is the creator of several seminars for The Center, including the *Writing to Learn* series and seminars based on the *Common Core State Standards for English Language Arts and Literacy*. Angela is a featured presenter at many of The Center's conferences, summits, and institutes and works both nationally and internationally.

Lisa Cebelak is The Leadership and Learning Center's ELA and Literacy Common Core Specialist. She has contributed to both of the Center's ELA Common Core seminar series, *ELA Common Core State Standards Overview* and *Getting to the Core of the Common Core State Standards for ELA—Rigor, Range, and Relationships.* Lisa is the cocreator of *Core Literacy*, a seminar on reading and writing strategies for all teachers to meet the rigor of the Common Core standards. She has also authored chapters for *Navigating the English Language Arts Common Core State Standards.* She has given keynote addresses in many states about the ELA and Literacy Common Core, and continues to research and write about this topic.

Lori Cook is a Professional Development Associate with The Leadership and Learning Center. She presents instruction on the *Five Easy Steps to a Balanced Math Program,* the Common Core State Standards, Data Teams, rigorous curriculum design, common formative assessments, and authentic performance assessments. Lori's passion is to help teachers perfect classroom instruction, which ultimately improves student learning and performance. Data analysis with ongoing formative assessment, in addition to the *Five Easy Steps to a Balanced Math Program,* significantly increased student performance in her high-risk urban mathematics classrooms. Lori has worked with many K–12 systems to improve the quality of math instruction to meet the new demands of the Common Core math standards. In addition to coaching elementary, middle, and high school teachers on effective math strategies, she has also guided K–12 curriculum teams through the rigorous curriculum design process. Student engagement and test scores have significantly increased as a result of increased rigor in teacher practices and student outcomes.

Lynn Howard is a Professional Development Associate with The Leadership and Learning Center and the author of *Ready for Anything* (2006) and *Five Easy Steps to a Balanced Science Program* (2010). She worked in the Charlotte-Mecklenburg School System in North Carolina for 30 years as a middle grades science teacher, gifted program coordinator, and Regional Assistant Superintendent. Lynn has presented for the Association of Middle Level Education, ASCD, National Science Teachers Association, International Reading Association, and Learning Forward, and has served on the National Association of Geoscience Education's National Speaker Bureau. She has a master's degree in earth science and education and has academy certification for the National Staff Development Council.

Lissa Pijanowski is a Professional Development Associate with The Leadership and Learning Center. Lissa has served as a public school educator for more than 22 years and most recently served as the Associate Superintendent of Academics and Accountability for Forsyth County Schools in Georgia. Her team was responsible for curriculum, instruction, assessment, academic support programs, professional learning, and workforce development. Lissa is passionate about promoting teaching, learning, and leadership through focused professional learning experiences and sustained implementation. Prior to working in Forsyth County Schools, Lissa served as the Director of School Improvement at the Georgia Department of Education, where she led regional school improvement teams to reduce the number of "Needs Improvement" schools in Georgia through intense training on data analysis, performance standards, and focused improvement planning. Lissa lives in Georgia with her husband and three children.

Ainsley Rose is a Professional Development Associate with The Leadership and Learning Center, with 41 years of experience in education. He is also an associate with Solution Tree and the Marzano Research Laboratory, and is the lead trainer for Visible Learning in North America. As the former director of education and curriculum for the Western Quebec School Board in Gatineau, Quebec, Canada, Ainsley was responsible for initiating many systemic changes that continue to impact teaching and learning there. Throughout his career as an education leader, Ainsley has incorporated his expertise in a wide range of principles, practices, and concepts into his work to significantly improve schools. Ainsley has pre-

sented across Canada, the United States, Bermuda, and Zambia on a range
of educational topics, including professional learning communities, instructional intelligences, Visible Learning, and standards and assessment.
Ainsley is married with three grown children and three grandchildren who
all live in the province of British Columbia.

Gabriel Rshaid has been an educator for almost 25 years, having taught
various subjects at the elementary and high school levels. For the last 15
years, he has been a K–12 principal in independent schools, while still remaining active in the classroom. Gabriel's passion for lifelong learning and
for technological developments has taken him on the intellectual journey
of thinking about education in the context of the new knowledge era and
considering how the 21st-century scenario of infinite knowledge can impact our lives decisively, which has led him to present in numerous venues
on the topics of 21st-century education and the future of learning. He currently resides in Buenos Aires, Argentina, with his wife and two sons.

Stephen Ventura is a Professional Development Associate with The Leadership and Learning Center and a former elementary, middle, and high
school teacher, assistant principal, principal, director, and superintendent.
Steve's work focuses on leadership strategies, data-driven decision making,
assessment, and standards and how they make the difference in quality
school improvement. In addition to his professional development work
with teachers and administrators, Steve is also a frequent speaker at state
and national conferences, and has contributed to several books focused
on teaching, learning, and leadership. Titles include *Standards and Assessment: The Core of Quality Instruction* (2011) and *Activate: A Leader's Guide
to People, Practices, and Processes* (2011).

David Nagel is a Senior Professional Development Associate with The
Leadership and Learning Center. A former middle school and high school
biology teacher, department chair, and administrator, his work has been
extensive in secondary education, specifically in grades 9–12. While working in his former district, the Metropolitan School District of Wayne

Township in Indianapolis, David was able to utilize his strengths in building collaborative teams and focusing on relationship-building with staff and students. During his tenure, the graduation rate at his high school rose by 14 percent in just over four years. As a Professional Development Associate with The Center, David's work consistently has been with high school teachers and leaders and he has helped them to adapt The Center's work to meet the needs of the comprehensive high school.

Sharon Bennett Delesbore is a Professional Development Associate with The Leadership and Learning Center. In her educational career, Sharon's experiences include teacher/coach, science instructional specialist, assistant principal, and principal. She holds active membership and leadership roles in Phi Delta Kappa, Omicron Delta Kappa, the National Science Teachers Association, and the Association for Multicultural Science Education. Sharon has a master's of education degree in curriculum and instruction in science education from the University of Houston.

What We Do Matters

Rachel Syrja

Déja vu. We've all experienced the feeling that we have been here before; that we have experienced these sensations, emotions, and feelings before. For many of us, the Common Core State Standards (CCSS) movement feels like this. Many educators experienced the first wave of standards in the 1990s and may be exclaiming, "Here we go again!" I would like to respectfully challenge that perception. If the CCSS are to truly prepare our students for the 21st century, we must not succumb to the temptation to continue doing what we've always done, only changing the test prep booklets we use each year. In *Navigating Implementation of the Common Core State Standards* (2011), Doug Reeves et al. take us back to the 1990s, when "... Hectares of trees were sacrificed as binders full of state standards documents were delivered to schoolhouse doors and then ... nothing. In many cases, classroom instruction and assessment was indistinguishable from the prestandards era" (p. 5). We have been given this amazing opportunity to push the "reset" button and begin anew with all the valuable lessons we've learned from our previous attempts at standards implementation. It provides us with the prospect of re-envisioning what instruction looks like in the era of the Common Core. The Leadership and Learning Center has been on the cutting edge of standards-driven instruction, curriculum, and assessment for the past two decades. As leaders in the field, they have invited experts from within the organization who represent every grade span and leadership position to contribute to this anthology. We've set out to provide teachers with concrete strategies and examples for helping us conceptualize what researchers mean when they say that instruction must change if we are to successfully prepare our students for the rigor of the CCSS.

There is no doubt that the challenges teachers face every day understandably leave them believing that there is little they can do to change the trajectory of the lives of their students. However, it is important to establish that this is far from the truth. John Hattie, in his groundbreaking book, *Visible Learning* (2009), writes, "Take two students of the same ability and it matters less to which school they go than the influences of the teacher, curricular program, or teaching they experience" (p. 18). More than ever, we know and can quantify the fact that what teachers do matters. Hattie goes on to show empirically that everything teachers do impacts student achievement, but that there are indeed some practices that work better than others. In our unending pursuit to find the best strategies to use with our students, Hattie challenges us to change our question from, "What works?" to "What works best?" This in turn guides our collaborative work so that we can sort out those strategies that have an effect that can be measured from those whose effects that are so obvious and clear that they are visible to the naked eye (Hattie, 2009, p. 8). While there is no question that teacher instincts and judgment play a significant role in the instructional decisions we make every day, research has shown us that they're not enough. With the advent of Common Core standards and the accountability that will accompany them (next generation assessments), there needs to be a shift towards using data as a basis for our instructional decisions versus solely relying on instincts and professional judgment.

This resource has been organized into three sections: Setting the Foundation to Prepare for the Common Core, Strategies in the Content Areas, and Strategies for Specialized Situations, ranging from strategies for English language learners to strategies for Response to Intervention (RTI). The chapters contained in these three sections present us with concrete strategies that we can implement immediately. If, as the research shows, the instructional decisions that a teacher makes each day are so critical, then our hope is to provide you with some research-based strategies that, when implemented deeply and differentiated appropriately to meet the needs of the students we teach, will make a difference and will begin to close the achievement gap now. The research and statistics presented on the following pages will reinforce that we, and more importantly our students, can't afford to wait any longer. If students are to have any hope of leaving our schools prepared for the challenges of the 21st century, then we need to get to work now. Let's take a closer look at the chapters you are about to explore.

Although we are more than a decade into it, in Part One, Gabriel Rshaid starts us off with a vision for education in the 21st century, also referred to as the age of information. He challenges us to make the leap ourselves and to teach our students the skills and concepts they require to be successful in this new era. In Chapter Two, Ainsley Rose reminds us that more than ever, collaboration is of the essence and presents us with a vision for becoming a true learning culture. John Almarode then takes us into the classroom and delves into student engagement and how we can no longer afford to allow the trend of rising dropout rates to continue. He presents us with staggering data that show that we are losing students in record numbers because they are not challenged and engaged in school, and points out that if we want to ensure that all students graduate from high school ready for college and careers, then changing the current trajectory of students at risk is a top priority. In Chapter Four, Stephen Ventura addresses the importance of strong leadership during this transition to the CCSS. He introduces us to the proven leadership practices that can take every school from learning about the Common Core to true deep implementation. Finally, Lissa Pijanowski introduces us to her "Five to Thrive" strategies to ensure that all students have an opportunity to learn in every classroom. She effectively makes a case for the importance of filling every teacher's toolbox with proven, research-based strategies.

Part Two takes us into the nuts and bolts of instructional practice, and the authors present us with strategies in four core content areas, writing, reading, math, and science. Angela Peery makes a compelling case for the teaching of argumentative writing, in particular, the importance of helping teachers define what argumentative writing is and how it differs from its cousin, persuasive writing. While many teachers believe that they are one and the same, Angela makes the important distinction between the two and then provides us with concrete strategies for teaching argumentative writing, beginning with opinion pieces in kindergarten. We learn about reading strategies from Lisa Cebelak in Chapter Seven, which describes strategies that encourage meaningful reading, which encourages critical thinking. She explains such key strategies as repeated reading, and illuminates the importance of such strategies in building students who are critical thinkers. In the following chapter, Lori Cook examines how the math classroom in the era of the Common Core needs to be highly engaging. She makes a compelling case for why math classes can no longer be teacher-centered and teacher-driven; she argues that they need to become places that require students to reason, interact with content and each other, and justify solutions. She also stresses that math needs to foster deep understanding of the mathematics students are learning rather than merely regurgitation of procedural steps. Lynn Howard and Sharon Delesbore close this section of the book with a peek into classrooms under the newly released Next Generation Science Standards. The theme of engagement is again presented in this chapter, along with strategies that ensure that science classrooms contain a balance of the essentials, including conceptual understanding of the standards, problem solving through research, demonstrations and experiments, and best instructional practices.

Part Three opens with my chapter on how instruction needs to change for English language learners (ELLs) in the era of the Common Core. I examine the conditions and strategies that can lead to increased learning and that can help ensure that we close the persistent achievement gap between ELLs and their native English-speaking peers once and for all. In Chapter Eleven, Tom Hierck, an expert in the area of Response to Intervention (RTI), continues by providing us with a vision for RTI in the era of the CCSS. He introduces us to strategies that bridge the gap between current practice and the desired outcomes to ensure learning for all. David Nagel takes on instruction at the high school level in Chapter Twelve. He makes the case for why education at the secondary level cannot just have positive effects, but instead needs to have exceptional effects. He walks us through the strategies that will increase student engagement, thus decreasing the dropout rate in secondary grades. Finally, Lynn Howard walks us through the importance of attracting and retaining the finest teachers, then introduces us to strategies for developing a new teacher program that does just that.

We stand at the precipice of what may prove to be our greatest moment—the moment when education in America no longer means that students are compared to other students, but are instead held to the same objective standards; the moment when rather than being sorted by ability, all students are held to the same rigorous standards and teachers work collaboratively to respond to the challenge of achievement gaps by providing strategically designed instructional opportunities to take students from where they are to where they need to be. The road will be long and hard, but armed with strategies like the ones outlined in the pages before you, we can make this vision a reality. Let's get to work!

References

Hattie, J. (2009). *Visible learning: A synthesis of over 800 meta-analyses relating to achievement.* New York, NY: Routledge.

Reeves, D., Wiggs, M., Lassiter, C., Piercy, T., Ventura, S., & Bell, B. (2011). *Navigating implementation of the common core state standards.* Englewood, CO: Lead + Learn Press.

PART ONE

Setting the Foundation to Prepare for the Common Core

CHAPTER ONE

Learning in the 21st Century

Gabriel Rshaid

Involuntarily, all educators are protagonists of one of the greatest paradoxes of modern history. Imagine if computer programmers, despite the breathtaking advances in processing capacity and speed, were still developing software using whole-room air conditioned mainframe computers fed by punched cards, while the rest of humanity went about their cosmetic use of computers with state-of-the-art powerful miniaturized devices. We find such a proposition absolutely ludicrous, yet this is, in a way, what happens with schools in the no-longer-so-new knowledge era.

The advent and generalization of the Internet opened up access to infinite information, and we are the first generation of learners to have full access to the whole array of accumulated human knowledge. Advances in miniaturization have enabled us to access the Internet as a source of knowledge continuously and ubiquitously. But despite these game-changing events, schools are still by and large operating within the same model as they did in the 19th century and are refusing stoically to embrace this new paradigm.

The reasons for this disconcerting disconnect are many and complex. Schools are extremely conservative businesses and do not easily embrace change; educators tend to have very rigid conceptions of what works and what does not. The well-trodden path to educational innovation (which, at this point, is almost an oxymoron) consists of research-based ideas that trust some form of comparable standardized measurements to yield classroom solutions that, more often than not, are in the form of one-size-fits-all strategies for teachers to universally apply to their students. This approach falls flat in the face of fast-paced changes, an intrinsically unstable and dynamic environment, and a future that is inherently unknown.

But the more profound reason why schools have not truly been able to transform themselves as required by the times is that the knowledge era requires a fundamental shift in mindset by all involved. Moving from a pedagogy of poverty, one that relies on the teacher as the one and only indispensable source of knowledge, to a pedagogy of infinite abundance, in which educators are catalysts and facilitators for learning, involves far more than just a change in the job description. Teachers are called out to rethink their roles so as to fundamentally shift the emphasis of the teaching and learning process from teaching to learning. This implies that there is a need for teachers to reassess their very reasons for being in the profession in the first place, and, essentially, to rekindle the learning dimension of their roles.

DEFINING THE CHALLENGE

The 21st-century challenge for educators can loosely be defined as to how to redefine schooling so that it can capitalize on the infinite learning possibilities that have opened up. The challenge entails developing a new pedagogy as well as teaching the new and unique skills that students need to deal with the overwhelming stimuli and tremendous complexity of a totally new learning landscape.

Even though we are well into the second decade of the 21st century already, the phrase "21st-century skills," largely used to denote the set of new skills that students need to learn, is well on its way into the well-populated graveyard of educational clichés, while at the same time it is still regarded as some distant, far-off proposition for the future. Despite this disconcerting state of affairs in education, focusing on the principles of the 21st-century challenge can provide a clear road map for learning for the future.

Being accustomed to the almost immutable principles that have served them well over, literally, centuries, educators find it hard to conceive that today the rhythm of change is so breathtakingly fast that even agreeing upon what student outcomes indicate success can be difficult. However, the basic principles of the new knowledge paradigm are irreversible, and provide a very solid foundation for understanding the extent and magnitude of the change required.

Lifelong Learning as the Primary Goal

Almost omnipresent in mission statements for schools regardless of age level, geography, and time, the quest for lifelong learning has traditionally been mostly well-intentioned wishful thinking. But educators have nonetheless been charged to develop this elusive skill in their students.

Continuous access to infinite knowledge just a few keystrokes away has dramatically changed that proposition; today, lifelong learning is not only a feasible reality, but also a fundamental goal of the educational system. Since learning is no longer restricted to access to formal schooling, providing students with the skills, the tools, and, most importantly, with the motivation to become life-long learners constitutes a major driver for a 21st-century school.

Shift from Teaching to Learning

As already hinted, another fundamental dimension of the challenge is related to converting our role from classroom instructors who are dispensing knowledge to that of colearners with our students. This allows, essentially, for the fact that the teacher is no longer the wisest person in the room. Weinberger (2012) explains this in terms of the emergence of a new form of knowledge: "As knowledge becomes networked, the smartest person in the room isn't the person standing at the front lecturing us, and isn't the collective wisdom of those in the room. The smartest person in the room is the room itself: the network that joins the people and ideas in the room, and connects to those outside of it."

Richardson (2012) also clearly addresses the need for teachers to become learners themselves: "There should also be no doubt that, to prepare students to be learners, we need adults in classrooms who can serve as outstanding role models for learning. If we're to develop learners who can make sense of the whole library, we must already be able to do that ourselves. In other words, the adults in the room need to be learners first and teachers second."

On top of all of the above, a renewed learning mindset can be the best antidote against unsettling change. When we look at changes through the prism of learning, the threat disappears and we can safely embrace change as the best catalyst for learning.

Every Child Can Learn

Even though there are so many dramatic changes to account for, the most important pedagogical finding of the 21st century is the realization that, indeed, any child can learn. In the previous model of schooling, the teacher's responsibility was limited to good delivery of content, and students were expected to perform to standards determined by the teacher, regardless of their learning styles and abilities. Even if it is still a distant reality, educators now understand that each and every child has a right to learn, that students have different learning styles and abilities, and that it is on the shoulders of the adults to find a way for all students to rise up to their full potential.

A Collaborative Environment

One of the greatest and most blatant disconnects of the current school system is related to the fact that, despite overwhelming evidence to the contrary, school is still largely designed for individual work and accountability. In the real world, in every order of activity, collaboration is the name of the game, and workers are expected to contribute effectively to teams, so much so that being a team player stands at the top of the list of desired traits in the workplace.

Our school system still caters mostly to the individual, and even when collaboration does occur, teachers painstakingly take care to make sure that team members do not hide within the group and shirk their duties. Thomas and Seely Brown (2012) make explicit reference to some of the underlying issues that result in this inexplicable miss:

> Take, for instance, one of the most difficult and dreaded classroom activities: the group project. Students struggle to

complete the exercise and teachers struggle to grade it. Why? Because our models of how a classroom works have no way of understanding, measuring, or evaluating collectives. Even worse, they have no means of understanding how notions of the personal may engage students. As a result, group work is almost always evaluated by assigning individual grades to students based on their contribution. What goes unrecognized is the fact that when groups work well, the result is usually a product of more than the sum of individual achievements. Even if a teacher does acknowledge that phenomenon and assign one grade to the entire group, the impulse is still to reward individual achievement (or in some cases punish the lack of it).

Technology as a Catalyst to Learning

From the early days of multimedia applications and CD encyclopedias, technology has been poised to revolutionize learning, but has not quite been effective in truly bringing forth a learning revolution. The reasons for this universally accepted failure are quite complex and are beyond the scope of this analysis, but one of the reasons why educational implementation has failed to deliver on technology's implicit promise to reinvent education is that the focus of most software and hardware applications for education is on teaching.

From the SMART board and the use of PowerPoint as a glorified blackboard to the document camera, most technological advances have reinforced the teacher-centered model of education.

Only recently, with the advent of ubiquitous iPads and other tablets, as well as increasing "1:1 laptop implementations" in schools, is technology slowly starting to be thought of as what it truly is—a catalyst for learning. Contrary to popular belief, the teachers who best utilize technology in the classroom are not the ones who are younger or more naturally drawn to it, but rather those who love learning themselves and cannot wait to share with their students the unlimited treasure chest of knowledge that lies just a Google search away.

Neuroscience

Even though it is still in its early research stages, specific knowledge about learning processes will continue to increase in ways that can eventually be translated into classroom activities. Although the "holy grail" of being able to access specific triggers to activate learning in the brain appears to still be a distant proposition, as more sophisticated imaging techniques evolve, there will be increasing amounts of knowledge available to assist teachers in a more brain-conscious pedagogy.

Neuroscience can bring forth revolutionary findings, since it would be almost the first time in the long history of human learning that educators would be assisted by knowledge about the inner mechanisms of the brain when they attempt to come up with more efficient learning strategies.

Ubiquitous Learning

One of the sacrosanct axioms of the old-school educational system was that learning occurred exclusively within the four walls of the school, and, with the exception of time-revered homework assignments, learning ceased the moment students traversed the classroom doorway. Thanks to Internet-connected devices that follow us everywhere and the realization that learning does not exclusively comprise the formal processes, learning is now, and will be even more so in the future, completely ubiquitous, leaving schools with the challenge of incorporating informal learning processes as a valid and valuable part of the curriculum.

Globalization

Another direct consequence of the advances in technology and telecommunications is the fact that educators face the challenge of making sense of a globally interconnected world that operates around the clock within an increasingly leveled playing field that enables not only unlimited interactions with other peoples and cultures but also the unprecedented challenge of having to compete in a global market. Incorporating a globalized dimension into education that truly targets international mindedness is no longer just a desirable boon, but rather a badly needed aspect of a well-rounded education.

Multimedia

Our loud protestations notwithstanding, with increased access to the Internet and better graphic capabilities in miniaturized connected devices, students are consuming more multimedia than they are traditional texts, as many related statistics attest. This is not to deny the undoubted benefits of continuing to have a strong reading and writing component in the curriculum, but schools must also acknowledge the fact that multimedia comprehension and production are necessary skills in the current context.

Skills Over Contents

This almost timeless eternal dilemma when it comes to curriculum design may very well have found its definitive resolution in the face of the need to learn completely new skills that stem naturally from the redefined knowledge paradigm. In the pre-Internet education model, where apprehending knowledge was essential, carefully concatenated contents in narrowly defined subject areas conformed to whatever external standards were in place. Skills were an afterthought, and, in many cases, some of the most necessary skills, such as critical thinking, were altogether omitted from the list of items explicitly referenced in the curriculum. Educators trusted that those essential skills would somehow be learned by students on automatic pilot. Content knowledge is now, by its very nature, almost transient, and knowledge as a fixed and immutable construct no longer exists. Weinberger (2012) goes as far as saying that "traditional knowledge has been an accident of paper." In this context, the traditional proposition is inverted and, surprisingly, content should now be chosen based on what is best-suited to allow for students to learn the skills they need, and not the other way around. This can be quite a difficult challenge, since it negates some of the basic instincts of educators, who always think of the content they need to teach first and foremost.

A 21st-CENTURY CURRICULUM

At first glance, the extent and magnitude of the change needed in our educational system is almost staggering, since many of the principles outlined above require more than revised methods and actually necessitate some deep shifts in the prevailing mindset regarding what is really important in education. However, even operating within existing constraints that are faced by educators every day in schools all over the world, a 21st-century curriculum can, indeed, be developed and deployed by targeting certain curriculum drivers and components that can gradually shift the collective teaching consciousness toward a more student-centered school model and that address the learning of new 21st-century skills.

Over the years, as educators increasingly became aware of the need for students to learn completely new skills in order to become proficient learners in the new knowledge paradigm, there were a myriad of attempts to come up with taxonomies to define and narrow the scope of those skills, with the view that they would serve as the starting point in the creation of a 21st-century curriculum. However, the very instability that is intrinsic to the 21st-century learning environment—the aforementioned fast-paced changes and advances in available technology for learning—renders those efforts almost futile.

Regardless of the taxonomies, it goes without saying that educators need to tap in to the tantalizing possibility of continuous access to infinite knowledge, and that doing so requires that students learn some completely new skills. Despite the uncertainty about the future of teaching and learning that has been repeatedly addressed as a defining characteristic of the 21st-century environment, some skills are here to stay, and will undoubtedly constitute some of the key skills needed to truly capitalize on the promise of a 21st-century education. They are the backbone of any 21st-century curriculum.

Filtering

If there were such a thing as a cornerstone of 21st-century skills, it would surely be the ability to filter the vast and overwhelmingly confusing amount of information available on the Internet that needs to be further processed and refined before it can be transformed into "knowledge." Filtering, in its basic form, can be defined as the set of tools and techniques required to be an effective Internet searcher.

The challenge is quite steep, since there are no barriers to self-proclaimed expertise. In the old days, when books were just about the only source of knowledge, there was at least an implicit assumption that, if something saw the light of day as a printed publication, it must have gone through some sort of screening process. The risk in the free-for-all Internet environment is that information found through a search engine might be incorrect, or even worse, biased or intentionally created to mislead potential readers for whatever reason.

There are two fundamental components to learning about filtering. First, students need to be able to discern the validity of sources they consult, so as to be able to decide what information they can trust. The most commonplace approach to doing this consists of students going to the Internet and navigating between different domain suffixes to try to distinguish between .org, .com, and so on, and sometimes also following some rules of thumb in terms of finding out who the author of the page is, the publishing organization, and so on. But this will only yield cosmetic results, and is entirely dependent on computer and Internet access. The best way to help students develop an essential instinctual sixth sense about which sites to trust or not can be developed from a very early age, and without the need for computers. In effect, students can be exposed in their assessments to biased or erroneous sources that they are expected to detect, or to out-of-range and clearly erroneous data in mathematics or science tests.

Another feature of assessment systems that conspires against students facing in school tests the same things they face in reality is that we tend to be extremely efficient and economical in the data we supply in our assessments. The norm is that problems and questions will always contain exactly as much data as needed, not one item more or less. In most cases, assessments should be refocused so that they contain more data than needed, as a way to foster the development of the skill of discerning which of the items included are actually needed and relevant to the solution of the problem.

The second aspect of filtering is related to learning specific search techniques. Searching for information effectively is such an important skill that it should not be left to students' own devices to acquire it; specific curricular activities should be included that target the intentional scientific learning of how to conduct effective Internet searches, with progressive intensity and levels of difficulty.

Critical Thinking

Another venerable component of wishful thinking mission statements for schools, critical thinking is no longer just a good to have skill, but an essential trait to be developed, because so much information needs to be decoded and interpreted. The fact that the Internet is open to anybody who fancies contributing their take on any subject makes critical thinking an indispensable skill for students to develop that will serve them well in the uncertain environments that they will have to face.

An Internet search yields a wealth of information about how critical thinking can be learned, as well as a myriad of lesson plans and other related resources to help catalyze the learning of the skill. Like many of the main drivers for a 21st-century curriculum, even though teaching critical thinking is not an exact science, attempting to create opportunities to address the skill is a very important first step.

Technological Literacy

To avoid engaging in fruitless categorization discussions, this heading includes all aspects of using technology for learning. In the same way that penmanship used to be an intrinsic part of any school curriculum when it came to written expression and, as such, was not only taught from a very tender age but also progressively monitored, to the point that students would not ever get away with producing a poorly presented piece of work with illegible handwriting, the use of technological devices is and will continue to be synonymous with learning.

The difference lies in the fact that the tool is infinitely more powerful and, as such, more complex to master in all its intricacies, and also that it opens up hitherto unthought-of possibilities and potential that need to be explicitly addressed within the school curriculum.

Paradoxically, the part of the learning process that generally concerns teachers the most—integrating technology—is the easiest one. Acquiring the tools to utilize technology efficiently seems to come as second nature to children, as Sugata Mitra's 1999 "Hole in the Wall" experiments can attest through their verified hypothesis that "the acquisition of basic computing skills by any set of children can be achieved through incidental learning provided the learners are given access to a suitable computing facility, with entertaining and motivating content and some minimal (human) guidance" (2012).

The really challenging part of computer literacy in the face of future technological developments that will challenge our assumptions regarding artificial intelligence, which is bound to surpass human intelligence at a point in time known in the field as "the singularity" (Kurzweil, 2006), is related to the personal and ethical implications of such advances. As young people lead increasingly rich and complex lives, new phenomena emerge, such as cyber-bullying, hacking, a certain cyber-schizophrenia where online acts are not held up to the same set of standards and values used to evaluate behavior in real life, attachment to robotic devices, and more; it is a long list of challenges, many of which are yet unknown.

As devices become more powerful and probe deeper into our personal lives, exposing our privacy and rendering us increasingly vulnerable, we cannot expect that the firms manufacturing those devices will provide us with guides to their ethical use. Their sole concern will be to increase sales of those products, and they will never hesitate to include more powerful features, even if they may prove to be controversial in their full application. It will be up to schools, once again, to provide a solid educational backbone on the ethical aspects of technology utilization.

Creativity

Creativity has long been hailed as the decisive skill in the new knowledge paradigm; however, very little is done in schools to address the learning of this quintessential 21st-century skill. The reason that creativity is more than just another skill to be acquired is that when so much content is available, the ability to see new connections, to innovate, and to be able to think in creative ways and find new uses for all that available information is what makes the difference.

The leveled playing field of the Internet is also propitious for the emergence of new and creative ideas, since there are no longer any obstacles between an individual or group of people and a global audience of millions.

In this context, creativity should not be relegated to implicit learning through the curriculum, but focused on through methodical, progressive, and increasing inclusion in the curriculum. Analyzing how to infuse creativity in the curriculum exceeds the scope of this analysis, but one simple example will suffice to illustrate that it is not difficult: Creativity can be encouraged by including questions in assessments with answers that are not just right or wrong but that allow for several plausible answers, and rewarding students for exercising their creativity and supplying as many reasonable answers as possible.

Other 21st-Century Curriculum Drivers

The building blocks of a 21st-century curriculum are not limited to the learning of 21st-century skills, and include many other interesting new paths for educators to tackle. These include developing a systematic and scientific body of knowledge regarding the decoding and production of multimedia; creating specific spaces for the development of imagination, a skill considered to be a precursor to creativity, and a skill that is certainly endangered by the current environment, in which everything can be visualized or simulated in stunning detail; transforming our schools to become eminently collaborative spaces; reconfiguring and re-creating physical spaces to facilitate a more participatory mode of learning; and, of course, other new principles that will appear as the learning landscape inevitably evolves.

A particularly interesting consideration regarding our environment of fast-paced changes is the ability to unlearn and relearn. Long declaimed as a sort of postmodern 21st-century education mantra, there is more to this than just the catchy phrase. One of the greatest difficulties that the older generation is having with the more transient nature of knowledge is the need to let go of old ideas and methods and truly be open to new and better ways of doing things. Like any skill and underlying mindset, school is the best place to learn this attitude of openness, which, beyond doubt, will serve students well now and in the future.

A 21st-CENTURY PEDAGOGY

As educators look into the future and try to reinvent themselves in the face of the challenge to prepare their students for a new and changing world of infinite knowledge, it is not enough to just create a new curriculum, however innovative it may turn out to be. It is also necessary to develop a whole new pedagogical approach, one that caters to the new curriculum and, essentially, to a completely new mode of learning.

Some characteristics of a 21st-century pedagogy include formative assessments that provide timely and relevant feedback, the teacher acting more as a facilitator and/or coach than an instructor, open-book assessments, use of freely available resources from the Internet whenever possible, and the utilization of technology not only to spur learning but also to engage students in a more participatory learning environment.

PROFESSIONAL DEVELOPMENT
IN THE 21st CENTURY

Professional development efforts are rightly focused on supplying educators with the tools and techniques needed to improve their practice, but that approach is not effective when there is a need to change more profound beliefs.

Work toward developing a new mindset cannot be immediate in its results, and a two-tiered approach is suggested. It is important to continue to emphasize the acquisition of new techniques, but it is equally important to increase the level of awareness of teachers as to the direction of the future of education and the need for teachers to rethink themselves and their learners, and also to provide teachers not only with learning instances but also with inspirational experiences that will indelibly imprint upon them the need and the imperative for the desired change.

A BETTER FUTURE

All in all, and despite the seemingly insurmountable challenges that educators face, we constantly need to remind ourselves that this is the best time in history to be educators. We have been given a blank knowledge check and the tools to make the best use of our newly acquired wealth. It is understandable that we may be tentative and even hesitant as we take our first steps toward this promised land, but the real key is to rethink our model of scarcity and adapt to one of abundance. Weinberger (2012) defines it for us: "This narrative focuses on preparing students to be learners, above all, who can successfully wield the abundance at their fingertips. It's a kind of schooling that prepares students for the world they will live in, not the one in which most of us grew up."

The famous opening line of the Charles Dickens classic *A Tale of Two Cities* comes to mind: "It was the best of times, it was the worst of times." That phrase parallels the reassessed emphasis within the teaching and learning process. This new era is seen by some to be the worst of times for teachers, but it is the best of times for learners. If we as educators re-evaluate our roles and think of ourselves as learners as well as teachers—as we must if we are to seek fulfillment in the 21st century—then it is the best of times for us all.

References

Kurzweil, R. (2006). *The singularity is near: When humans transcend biology.* New York, NY: Penguin.

Mitra, S. (2012). *Beyond the hole in the wall: Discover the power of self-organized learning.* Amazon Kindle Single. TED Books.

Richardson, W. (2012). *Why school? How education must change when learning and information are everywhere.* Amazon Kindle Single. TED Books.

Thomas, D., & Seely Brown, J. (2011). *A new culture of learning: Cultivating the imagination for a world of constant change.* CreateSpace Independent Publishing Platform.

Weinberger, D. (2012). *Too big to know: Rethinking knowledge now that the facts aren't the facts, experts are everywhere, and the smartest person in the room is the room.* New York, NY: Basic.

CHAPTER TWO

The Importance of Instruction in Becoming a Learning Culture

Ainsley B. Rose

"We spend far too much time talking about particular methods of teaching. The debate seems so often to centre on this or that method: we have had battles about direct instruction, constructivism, cooperative versus individualistic teaching, and so on. Our attention, instead, should be on the effect we have on student learning— and sometimes we need multiple strategies and, more often, some students need different teaching strategies from those they have been getting."

JOHN HATTIE, 2012, p. 83

With the introduction of the Common Core State Standards and the general and rather widespread commitment to implementing these standards, there is reason to think that something might be different about schools in the future if these standards are adopted in classrooms across the country. Will it be how teachers teach? Will it be what they teach, and at what point they teach it? How and what will teachers assess and evaluate? To what degree will the curriculum be covered? Will students achieve the more rigorous standards? Will they be college- and career-ready? Will increasing numbers of students be ready? How will the United States do in the international assessments as a result of these new standards?

All these questions, while interesting, are not any different than the questions we have asked for decades. For me, the most important *new* question is: how will teaching be different from what it is now? Indeed, *will* teaching be different, and what is it going to take to help teachers see instruction from a new perspective? Finally, and perhaps most importantly, what mechanisms currently exist in schools and districts to help teachers acquire the skills and competencies needed for the implementation of this new more rigorous and demanding curriculum?

The Common Core State Standards documents offer standards, but not strategies. "The best understanding to what works in the classroom comes from the teachers who are in them. That's why these standards will establish *what* students need to learn, but they will not dictate *how* teachers should teach. Instead, schools and teachers will decide how best to help students reach those standards" (Daggett and Gendron, 2010, p. 4). Joyce and Weil add that "how teaching is conducted has a large impact on students' abilities to educate themselves . . . thus a major role in teaching is to create powerful learners" (1996, p. 7).

The implications are onerous for a variety of people within districts and in particular schools. Daggett and Gendron emphasize this point: "Leaders must begin building instructional capacity within their systems in order to ensure successful roll-out of the new standards and assessments. Schools and districts will need a focused transition plan and a process to implement the plan" (2010, p. 8).

A LEARNING CULTURE

The title of this chapter suggests an orientation to some of the popular notions currently in vogue in schools. Terms such as communities of practice, learning organizations, professional learning communities, and learning culture have many similarities. Common to all is the notion that everyone in the organization becomes a learner. Both adults and students alike need to exist in an environment that is very unlike our present school paradigm: a place where students go to watch adults work, or a place where teachers, as independent consultants, are joined together by a common parking lot. So, it is important that leaders and ultimately teachers take into account that in order to be successful in this "last ditch effort" to put the U.S. back in the "game," as it were, changes will need to be made. Daggett and Gendron (2010, p. 9), also draw attention to this notion:

> The implications for educators of the Common Core State Standards are both exciting and daunting. Educators will need to shift how they teach and how they assess students within the next three years. Students will need to adapt to those instructional changes and cannot be expected to do so overnight. The transition to new standards and assessments will require vision, gaining commitment and consensus, planning time, and increased instructional capacity to support teachers in developing an expanded repertoire of skills in anticipation of these new measurements of achievement.

The implication is that we need to create a "culture of learning" in schools and districts. A learning culture is more than what happens between teachers and students. While one could argue this daily dance is the core of the work in schools, clearly there is more involved in this complex interplay of adults and youth. Senge et al. (2000) support this point when they say, "Classrooms can only improve in a sustainable way if schools around them improve. Schools depend on the districts and communities of which they are a part … in our view, a learning school is not so much a separate place (for it may not stay in one place) as a meeting ground for learning—dedicated to the idea that all those involved with it, individually and together, will be continually enhancing and expanding their awareness and capabilities" (p. 6).

Improving schools is dependent on improving the culture of those schools and communities in which they reside. As Sergiovanni (1996) indicates, "Culture is important in improving schools. Less obvious is the connection between culture and theory. The heart and soul of school culture is what people believe, the assumptions they make about how schools work, and what they consider to be true and real" (p. 3).

The best definition of culture that I have come across is credited to Robert Sternberg (2007), who says, "Culture is the set of attitudes, values, beliefs and behaviors shared by a group of people, communicated from one generation to another via language or some other means of communication." Clearly, this is a broad definition that applies to a greater scope than the school or classroom. It does, however, give us substance on which to define what culture means in terms of a learning culture. The essence of Sternberg's definition deals with the "set of attitudes, values, beliefs and behaviors shared by a group of people." Schools certainly fit this description.

EFFECT OF INSTRUCTION ON CULTURE

We have to consider the complexities of the environment of schools and classrooms: the orchestration of personalities, beliefs, and values; the preconceptions of students and teachers; and principals with mandates from governments, parent groups, and communities at large. All these bodies of thought shape what goes on in the classroom, concurrent with the dramatic interplay of teacher, student, curriculum, assessment, instruction, and evaluation methods. So, to isolate teaching or instruction is somewhat dangerous and maybe even naïve. Having said that, I still believe that instruction is clearly one of the most important factors, if not the most important factor.

Hattie, in his now celebrated work *Visible Learning: A synthesis of over 800 meta-analyses relating to achievement* (2009), identifies some 150 different influences clustered in six different themes that help to inform us about the impact of various influences on learning and student achievement. Among the top influences, instruction is not actually listed as a separate category. However, aspects of instruction, such as feedback, Piagetian programs, providing formative evaluation, teacher clarity, direct instruction, and microteaching, are certainly components of the instructional process and therefore essential when talking about a "learning culture."

In *Visible Learning for Teachers* (2012), Hattie goes on to say, "It matters what teachers do—but what matters most is having an appropriate mind frame relating to the impact of what they do" (p. 15). The members' mind frames, then, are the essence of a group's culture. What we bring to our work is a function of our beliefs, attitudes, and values. Organizations, therefore, reflect or mirror the beliefs, attitudes, and values of the people within them. They work the way they work because of the way people in those organizations think about their work (Senge, et al., 2000). This presents a huge challenge, as it is no small feat to get people to have similar perspectives about learning and teaching. So, if we want to improve the systems (schools), before we do so, we need to be mindful of how the people within those systems work together and how they think the same or differently on a myriad of issues, not the least of which is what they think about instruction. Senge et al. (2000) make a really interesting point when they say, "Too often, classrooms, professional development in schools and other organizations, parenting classes, and teacher or school leadership preparation programs focus only on two factors in learning—what is covered and how it is delivered" (p. 21). This suggests to me that in thinking about creating a culture of instruction, it is clearly not sufficient to just think about teaching; it is also necessary—even imperative—to consider the environment in which it occurs.

THE DATA TEAMS PROCESS

Yet, there are examples of successful strategies in creating environments in schools to establish a culture of expectation that all students can and will learn. The Data Teams process, espoused for years by The Leadership and Learning Center, is one such process that is designed to engage teachers in a step-by-step process, one step of which is germane to our topic. Step four is about determining the appropriate and deliberate instructional strategies to be used in light of the effect data (student results) the team of teachers in any given Data Team is examining. The Data Teams process steps, while important, are effective not so much because of the process as because of the conversations and results the teachers arrive at that help determine future practice in the classroom. Teachers adjust their instructional approach first by selecting an appropriate instructional strategy or two and then by applying those strategies in the classroom and assessing the effects of those strategies through common formative assessments. They are now in a better position to determine the strategies' impact through evidence of better student results.

Hattie (2012) says that "one of the more successful methods for maximizing the impact of teaching and enabling teachers to talk to each other about teaching is direct instruction" (p. 65). For more detailed information about the direct instruction method, and to avoid confusing it with didactic teaching, I recommend that you read Chapter 4 in Hattie's *Visible Learning for Teachers* (2012) to gain a comprehensive understanding of the process.

INSTRUCTIONAL INTELLIGENCE

Hattie (2012) helps to affirm the need for team-driven data-based decision making in the classroom when he says, "The single greatest issue that we identified was the need for teachers to have a common understanding of progress" (p. 58). I would add that it is equally important for students to have a picture of what progress looks like while learning is occurring. Suffice to say that this is integral to the instructional process, or as Bennett and Rolheiser (2001) call it, "instructional intelligence." They claim that "knowledge of instruction—as one component or thread in the teaching and learning process—can assist in responding to the never-ending press to create meaningful and powerful learning environments. This implies creative instruction; it implies an ever-deepening understanding of subject knowledge" (p. 4).

Instructional intelligence means the extent to which teachers are intelligent about their instructional behaviors. Instruction is not just about designing clever or engaging activities. Rather, it involves being intelligent about how to best use the skills, tactics, concepts, strategies, and organizers that are utilized to make the decisions that teachers must make when approaching the design and application in their teaching of a unit of instruction. Teachers must be purposeful and thoughtful about designing learning situations by combining the various methods to best meet the needs of students. Instructional intelligence is about the ability of teachers to combine low-power strategies, skills, and tactics with high-power strategies, skills, and tactics to create the appropriate conditions for the students most in need of those particular skills, tactics, and strategies depending on where they are in their learning. Knowing what constitutes a strategy, skill, tactic, concept, or organizer is the "science" of instruction, whereas, knowing which of these various elements to use in a given situation for a particular student, and how to blend them together, is the "art" of instruction.

Despite the importance of teachers recognizing when and how to use the various components of good instruction, this thinking falls somewhat short as far as Hattie is concerned. He implores us to be more thoughtful about which methods or strategies we choose: "Various methods of teaching were identified in *Visible Learning*, but the book also identified the importance of not rushing to implement only the top strategies; rather it is important to understand the underlying reasons for the success of the strategies and use this as basis for making decisions about teaching methods" (2012, p. 84).

The message is that it is important to determine which of the methods chosen has the greatest impact on whether students learn or not. Better yet, determine which students have shown growth as a result of choosing a particular instructional method. This drives home the complexity of good instruction. And attempting to create a learning culture along the way adds to this complexity.

INSTRUCTIONAL DESIGN

Marzano (2007) writes that good instruction is based on sound science and research. His framework for instruction is best illustrated by the 10 instructional design questions he proposes that teachers use to create a logical planning sequence for engaging and purposeful lessons:

- What will I do to establish and communicate learning goals, track student progress, and celebrate success?
- What will I do to help students effectively interact with new knowledge?
- What will I do to help students practice and deepen their understanding of new knowledge?
- What will I do to help students generate and test hypotheses about new knowledge?
- What will I do to engage students?
- What will I do to establish or maintain classroom rules and procedures?
- What will I do to recognize and acknowledge adherence and lack of adherence to classroom rules and procedures?
- What will I do to establish and maintain effective relationships with students?

- What will I do to communicate high expectations for all students?
- What will I do to develop effective lessons organized into a cohesive unit?

In examining these questions, the complexity of the instructional process becomes quite evident. If I were to suggest one small amendment to Marzano's list of questions it would be to change the pronoun used from "I" to "we" throughout. I suggest this to make it clear that it is in the collective and collaborative discussion and dialogue between and among all teachers that we gain the leverage to get better at the instructional process—particularly given the inherent complexity of planning and implementing the strategies and processes that are evident in the list above. The complexity of instruction and the strain it puts on teachers is one of the reasons that creating a learning culture remains an elusive goal. As Hattie says, "Teachers don't mind change; they are not so happy about being changed" (2012, p. 84).

Herein lies the essence of developing a learning culture among teachers in a school and district. To think that a teacher is able to do all this in isolation is sheer folly. Teachers and principals need to engage in ongoing dialogue with their peers to achieve any semblance of "instructional intelligence." As Hattie contends, "The best way in which to choose the best teaching method (and the way in which to change teachers so that they begin to use the best method) is to place more attention on the evaluation of the learning effect sizes from the lesson, and use these as the first discussion point for considering whether the optimal teaching methods have been used" (p. 86).

Bennett and Rolheiser (2001) propose that the best way to implement these methods in classrooms and schools is to marry the strategy of professional development in teaching methods with a model of systemic change.

There are many models, such as the aforementioned Data Teams model, that are designed to examine the impact of instruction. Others, such as "instructional rounds" (City, Elmore, Fiarman, and Teitel, 2009) and the Response to Intervention model, all purport to examine instruction as the determining factor in improving student learning. In every instance, the effectiveness of these approaches lies in the extent to which the teachers who form these teams engage in collaborative conversations designed to examine the impact they are having on student learning and achievement (Hattie, 2012).

PROFESSIONAL LEARNING COMMUNITIES

As previously noted, *one* approach to systemic change that has proved to be effective and lasting is the professional learning communities framework. Senge et al. (2000) concur: "The idea of a school that can learn has become increasingly prominent during the last few years. It is becoming clear that a school can be recreated, made vital, and sustainable, renewed not by fiat or command, and not by regulation, but by taking a learning orientation. This means everyone in the system is expressing their aspirations, building their awareness and developing their capabilities together" (p. 5). Earlier approaches to creating learning organizations were couched in terms such as effective schools, school reform, organizational development, and similar notions of systemic change models. Common to all the models was the imperative for people to work and talk together about their practices and about the practices necessary to creating an environment conductive to success for all.

"The culture of most school faculties has been highly individualistic, with nearly all interaction over day-to-day operations. Without collective action, schools have difficulty addressing problems that cannot be solved by individual action. Without a balance between operations and the study of teaching and curriculum, the school is liable to drift toward obsolescence and fail to adapt to the needs of surrounding society. Reorienting school cultures toward collegial problem solving and the study of advances in research on curriculum and teaching is vitally important (Schon, 1982)" (Joyce and Weil, 1996, p. 376).

Devotees of the professional learning communities (PLCs) model have long advocated that schools need to shift their emphasis from a culture of teaching to a culture of learning. At the same time, there has been a reluctance to talk about teaching at all from those well schooled in PLC parlance. Yet, we all know that instruction drives learning. More to the point, it is the *quality* and *impact* of instruction that drive learning.

PLCs are predicated on three ideas from the effective school literature:

1. All staff work on collaborative teams

2. Shift the paradigm from one of teaching to one of learning

3. Data drives the conversation

Furthermore, when teams are formed and do their collaborative work, they do so with a focus on four essential questions to frame their regular meetings. Those questions are (Dufour, Dufour, Eaker, and Many, 2006):

1. What do we want all students to learn?

2. How will we know they have learned?

3. What will we do when they don't learn?

4. What will we do if they already know what we want them to learn?

I suggest that to make PLCs work, one must consider the instructional component as both necessary and essential for higher levels of learning for students and for teachers. So, I suggest a fifth question:

5. How do we teach in order for students to learn?

I believe that question is critical. When a lesson does not go as it should, how do teachers find out what it is about the lesson that did not go well, and on what basis do they determine that it did not go well? They do not want to repeat the same behaviors that led to the ineffective lesson. There is a need to deconstruct the lesson, and in doing so, to examine all the elements in the instructional process to determine what needs to change. As Bennett and Rolheiser (2001) say, "Too often we hear of teachers throwing out an innovation after trying it once or twice. Yet, talking with them revealed that the problem related to another issue that they did not consider connected to the effective implementation of the innovation" (p. 14). Teachers need to consider how what they do is interconnected, which can lead to outcomes they had not anticipated in designing the lesson in the first place.

While learning for students is clearly the goal, surely what affects this learning must undergo the same scrutiny we give the other four PLC questions. Joyce and Weil (1996) help us understand this notion more deeply; "The message is that the most effective teachers [and designers] need to master a range of models and prepare for a career-long process of adding new tools and polishing and expanding their old ones" (p. 25).

A CULTURE FOR SUCCESS

The success of the Common Core State Standards depends on the degree to which districts, schools, principals, and teachers agree that a new approach to implementing change is needed. We often hear the refrain that doing the same thing and expecting different results is the definition of insanity. Let's learn from past failures and take the opportunity to build from an optimistic perspective and create the conditions that will make the difference for all students and teachers. Joyce and Weil (1996, p. 375), said it best:

> It is plain from the research on training that teachers can be wonderful learners. They can master just about any kind of teaching strategy or implement almost any kind of sensible curriculum—if the appropriate conditions are provided. It is also clear that those who criticize the motivations of teachers, worry about their willingness and ability to learn, or believe that the only way to improve the teaching profession is to change its personnel, are fundamentally wrong.

As instruction is primarily the domain of the classroom teacher, let us create the "appropriate conditions" to which Joyce and Weil refer and build a culture that will allow instruction to be at the heart of what teachers do—and do to the highest level—regardless of the curriculum to which they are assigned.

I end where I began. The most important new questions in the face of the Common Core are: How will teaching be different from what it is now? Indeed, *will* teaching be different, and what is it going to take to help teachers see instruction from a new perspective? Finally, what mechanisms currently exist in schools and districts to help teachers acquire the skills and competencies needed for the implementation of this new more rigorous and demanding curriculum?

It is up to each school system to answer these questions. It is apparent that classroom instruction must change to reflect Common Core demands. The question now is, will schools step up to meet the challenge? Teachers want their students to learn, and given the proper tools and the right environment, they will surmount any obstacle to achieve that goal. Existing collaborative models, such as the Data Teams process and professional learning communities, can help to foster a culture of learning in which educators embrace changes that can enable students to achieve the lofty ideal of college and career readiness.

References

Bennett, B., & Rolheiser, C. (2001). *Beyond Monet: The artful science of instructional integration.* Toronto, ON: Bookation.

City, W., Elmore, R., Fiarman, S., & Teitel, L. (2009). *Instructional rounds in education: A network approach to improving teaching and learning.* Cambridge, MA: Harvard Educational Press.

Daggett, W., & Gendron, S., (2010, August). *Common Core State Standards Initiative: Classroom implications for 2014.* International Center for Leadership in Education. www.LeaderEd.com

Dufour, R., Dufour, R., Eaker, B., & Many, T. (2006). *Learning by doing: A handbook for professional learning communities at work.* Bloomington, IN: Solution Tree.

Hattie, J. (2009). *Visible learning: A synthesis of over 800 meta-analyses relating to achievement.* London: Routledge.

Hattie, J. (2012). *Visible learning for teachers: Maximizing impact on learning.* London: Routledge.

Joyce, B., & Weil, M. (1996). *Models of teaching* (5th ed.). Boston, MA: Allyn and Bacon.

Marzano, R. (2007). *The art and science of teaching: A comprehensive framework for effective instruction.* Alexandria, VA: ASCD.

Schön, D. (1982). *The reflective practioner: How professionals think in practice.* New York, NY: Basic Books.

Senge, P., Cameron-McCabe, N., Lucas, T., Smith, B., Dutton, J., & Kleiner, A. (2000). *Schools that learn: A fifth-discipline fieldbook for educators, parents and everyone who cares about education.* New York, NY: Doubleday.

Sergiovanni, T. (1996). *Leadership for the schoolhouse: How is it different? Why is it important?* San Francisco, CA: Jossey-Bass.

Sternberg, R. (2007, February). Culture, instruction, and assessment. *Comparative Education* (special issue 33), *43*(1), 5–22.

CHAPTER THREE

Student Engagement

John Almarode

"To teach is to engage students in learning; thus teaching consists of getting students involved in the active construction of knowledge. A teacher requires not only knowledge of subject matter but also knowledge of how students learn and how to transform them into active learners. Good teaching, then, requires a commitment to systematic understanding of learning ... The aim of teaching is not only to transmit information, but also to transform students from passive recipients of other people's knowledge into active constructors of their own and others' knowledge."

KARL SMITH, 2000, p. 25

THE PROBLEM

According to a report released by the National Center for Education Statistics (2012), approximately 8,300 students drop out of America's high schools per school day. This number translates into approximately one student every 11 seconds making the decision to walk away from our classrooms to pursue what they feel are more appealing opportunities, despite the fact that data suggest there are expensive consequences to this decision: students who drop out are more likely to be unemployed, live in poverty, experience ill health, be incarcerated, and seek support from social services (Alliance for Excellent Education, 2009; Balfanz and Neild, 2007; Allensworth and Easton, 2005). Financially, America's estimated total economic loss over the lifetime of each dropout class is 90 billion dollars (Levin, Belfield, Muennig, and Rouse, 2007; Rouse, 2005). These troubling statistics beg the question: why are so many of America's students choosing options other than earning a high school diploma each year in the United States? Put differently, why would someone take their chances with unemployment, poverty, ill health, incarceration, and social programs instead of staying in school and earning a high school diploma? Are America's classrooms that unwelcoming?

Researchers have long sought a solution to America's dropout problem, and in many cases, schools seek a magic bullet, or the be-all-and-end-all solution to preventing students from exiting our classrooms without earning their diplomas (e.g., Academy of Creative Education, Admission Possible, and CASASTART [Striving Together to Achieve Rewarding Tomorrows]). A perfect solution has yet to be identified for all of America's students who are at risk for dropping out. However, researchers have identified variables or factors that are correlated with the students dropping out of school, such as minority status, poverty, and low test scores (Gleason and Dynarski, 2002). What is interesting about many of these variables or factors correlated with students dropping out of school is that these variables are not predictive of whether students will actually drop out (Rumberger, 2004). This makes sense and may not be surprising to many district leaders, building administrators, and teachers. For example, many schools and school systems have a majority of students that share these characteristics and have graduation rates that exceed the national average. A student being classified as an ethnic minority, poor, or not performing well on tests does not mean that the student will make the decision to not graduate from high school.

What characteristics or factors do serve as predictors of students dropping out of school and ultimately answer the question, why do students drop out of school? A growing body of research is beginning to answer this question. As a result, schools are developing more effective interventions by identifying variables or factors that are predictive of a student dropping out of school rather than simply being correlated with students who exit America's schools too soon. Predictors of dropping out include attendance, behavior, course performance, disrupted lifestyle (e.g., death of a parent, homelessness, becoming pregnant while in school), boredom, lack of relevancy, and being pushed out by suspension and expulsion (Jerald, 2006; Rumberger, 2004 and 1995; Allensworth and Easton, 2005; Balfanz and Legters, 2004; Roderick and Camburn, 1999; Bridgeland, DiIulio, and Morison, 2006). One salient feature of this list of predictors is the number of factors that extend beyond the reach of the school district, the school these students attend, and the classrooms in which they sit. Given the research on the characteristics associated with school dropout and the factors that are predictive of school dropout, district leaders, building administrators, and classroom teachers would be justified in feeling a sense of helplessness and hopelessness when it comes to addressing America's dropout problem, much less solving it. After all, we have no control over a student's race, ethnicity, socioeconomic status, or lifestyle.

However, studies on why students drop out of school that include interviews from students that made the choice to walk away from school reveal a common factor that is well within the control of district leaders, building administrators, and, most importantly, classroom teachers (Bridgeland, DiIulio, and Morison, 2006; Balfanz and Neild, 2007; Allensworth and Easton, 2005; Rumberger, 1995 and 2004). This common factor is student engagement. In all of the studies involving student interviews, a common thread in each dropout's response was that classes were not interesting, they did not like school, or they did not find learning relevant (Bridgeland, DiIulio, and Morison, 2006; Rumberger, 1995 and 2004). All students included in these studies expressed some level of disengagement with the school, classroom, and/or teacher. In fact, Rumberger (2004) found that above and beyond student background variables and prior academic achievement, student engagement is a very strong predictor of dropping out.

Similarly, the 2009 High School Survey of Student Engagement (HSSSE) conducted by the Center for Evaluation and Education Policy at Indiana University reported that 66 percent of students surveyed indicated that they were bored on at least a daily basis, 49 percent reported they were bored every day, and 17 percent of the respondents reported they were bored in every class (Yazzie-Mintz, 2010). Similar to earlier findings (e.g., Bridgeland, DiIulio, and Morison, 2006; Rumberger, 1995 and 2004), HSSSE found that respondents attributed their reported boredom to the material not being interesting, lack of relevance in the material, the work not being challenging enough, the work being too challenging, and limited student-teacher relationships (Yazzie-Mintz, 2010). How does this connect to the dropout problem? The HSSSE also found that students who reported that they considered dropping out of school did so because they did not like school, did not see value in what they were being asked to do in school, or did not like their teachers. This further highlights Rumberger's (2004) findings that above and beyond student background variables and prior academic achievement, student engagement is a strong predictor of dropping out.

THE SOLUTION: STUDENT ENGAGEMENT

Students spend approximately 30 percent of their waking time in school. From kindergarten to twelfth grade, this adds up to about 13,000 hours (Jensen, 2005 and 2009). As research has continued to demonstrate, school-level, classroom-level, and teacher-level factors are associated with and predictive of students' decision to drop out of school (Bridgeland, DiIulio, and Morison, 2006; Yazzie-Mintz, 2010). These factors fall under the overarching concept of student engagement. Given that these engagement factors are related to instructional content and material as well as student-teacher relationships, the most immediate and relevant action that we can take as classroom teachers is to focus on student engagement, something that is well within our control. Simply put, it is all about engagement.

The decision of a student to disengage from what is happening in the classroom and then school in general is something that does not happen during a single day or school year. Instead, disengagement is a process that evolves as a result of years of experiences (Christenson, Sinclair, Lehr, and Godber, 2001). Engagement, on the other hand, can be sparked immediately based on the environmental conditions of a single K–12 classroom or the actions and decisions of a teacher (Almarode and Miller, 2013). Student engagement is both a relevant and an essential component of teaching and learning across the K–12 spectrum. That is, even though high schools catch much of the attention with regard to the dropout problem, it is important that student engagement remains the centerpiece of teaching and learning during all points of the students' educational trajectory.

WHAT IS STUDENT ENGAGEMENT?

Engagement is a multidimensional concept (Fredricks, Blumenfeld, and Paris, 2004; Appleton, Christenson, and Furlong, 2008; Reschly, Huebner, Appleton, and Antaramian, 2008; Skinner, Kinderman, and Furrer, 2009). Specifically, in the classroom, a student engages in instructional content, material, and learning activities in three ways: 1) his or her personal feelings about the content, material, and learning activity; 2) his or her behaviors or actions while in the classroom; and 3) what he or she is thinking about while in the classroom. Student engagement includes emotional engagement (how the student feels), behavioral engagement (the behaviors or actions of the student), and cognitive engagement (what the student is thinking). How we as teachers set up our classrooms has a major influence on both the type and level of engagement of the students on a daily basis (Almarode and Miller, 2013). Consider the following three scenarios:

1. Mrs. Smith, an algebra 2 and trigonometry teacher, has a procedure for everything. The students walk into the room at the beginning of each period, quickly take their seats, and before the tardy bell

rings, start on the warm-up exercise for the day. Approximately five minutes after the tardy bell, Mrs. Smith moves to the front of the room and begins to go over the problems from the warm-up exercise and then moves into the day's content by working several example problems. The students quietly and furiously take notes, being careful to copy down each step involved in the worked examples. This continues for much of the class. Mrs. Smith has a reputation for having excellent classroom management. Each time her principal does a classroom walkthrough, she is commended for how all of her students are so well-behaved.

2. Mr. Jones, a middle school U.S. history teacher, is one of the most well-liked teachers in the school. As a U.S. history teacher, Mr. Jones works very hard to tie concepts in his class to current events. He does this by using documentaries, movies, and games. For example, on Nov. 22, he shows an hour-long documentary on the Kennedy assassination, and on April 14, he shows the movie *A Night to Remember* for the anniversary of the sinking of the RMS Titanic. In addition to movies and documentaries, Mr. Jones creates copious games around historical facts and information. Each time his principal does a classroom walkthrough, he is commended for his special ability to make learning fun.

3. Mrs. Taylor, a fourth-grade teacher, has high expectations for her students. She believes that pushing

students to reach their potential is very important for their success. Mrs. Taylor fills up every single second of the day with instructional content. From the time the students enter the room at 8:15 a.m. until the time they load the buses at 3:06 p.m., Mrs. Taylor is presenting new content to her students. In language arts and mathematics, Mrs. Taylor addresses all of the Common Core State Standards. In science, Mrs. Taylor has already adjusted her unit plans to meet the Next Generation Science Standards. Each time her principal does a classroom walkthrough, she is commended for her strenuous pace and content-driven classroom. "Mrs. Taylor has those students working hard all of the time."

The ideal classroom strikes a balance between emotional, behavioral, and cognitive engagement every day, adjusting this balance based on careful monitoring of the students through observations, interaction, and feedback. Each of the three scenarios above is an example of a classroom where student engagement is out of balance. In scenario one, Mrs. Smith's classroom is heavy on behavioral engagement, but she is unaware of what her students are feeling about the material or what they are thinking about while copying down the worked examples. Let's be honest: students can copy notes all day long while thinking about other things and not feeling very good about the content. These students are likely to report that the material is not interesting, lacks relevance, and is not challenging enough. These students will also likely report that they have a less-than-productive student-teacher relationship (Yazzie-Mintz, 2010). After all, it is hard to connect with students or for students to connect with you if your entire class is spent in front of the chalkboard.

In scenario two, Mr. Jones' classroom is heavy on emotional engagement, but he is unaware of what his students are doing or thinking during the documentaries and movies. Unless a specific task is assigned during a documentary or movie, what students do or think about when the lights are out is a gamble. Similarly, games are fun but may not encourage students to think about the concepts in a way that is necessary for them to develop the required level of understanding. Furthermore, students who simply want to win will not be as concerned about the material, while students who lose may disengage entirely. These students are likely to report that the material lacks relevance (all we do is watch movies and play games) or is not challenging enough (Yazzie-Mintz, 2010), and when assessed, students may find that they do not know the material.

In scenario three, Mrs. Taylor's classroom is heavy on cognitive engagement. Although a focus on standards is both a necessary and sufficient condition for student achievement, the students' brains cannot maintain a continuous flow of information without opportunities to process and reflect. Once the students' brains reach their threshold for new information in a given period, they no longer have the physical resources or the working memory capacity to make new memories or store temporary ones (Abel and Lattal, 2001; Bliss and Collingridge, 1993; Cowan, 2001; Kandel, 1997; Miller, 1956; Nilsson, Radeborg, and Björck, 2012; Silva, 2003; Smith and Foster, 2008; Squire, 1992; Squire and Cave, 1991). Teaching more content does not mean students will learn more content. In this scenario, the students will ultimately cognitively disengage simply because their brains are tired. These students are likely to report that the material is not interesting, lacks relevance, and is too challenging, and that there are strained student-teacher relationships (Yazzie-Mintz, 2010).

AN EMOTIONALLY, BEHAVIORALLY, AND COGNITIVELY ENGAGING ENVIRONMENT

The take-home message from these three scenarios is that student engagement is multidimensional—emotional, behavioral, and cognitive—with each dimension playing an important role in maintaining overall student engagement within our classrooms. Devoting too much attention to one particular type of engagement and neglecting the other two will not produce the desired outcomes for our students.

To foster and nurture an environment that maximizes student engagement, teachers should utilize strategies and design learning activities that actively engage students behaviorally, emotionally, and cognitively. What this looks like on a daily basis will depend on the students. Some days will require more attention to emotional engagement, while other days will require more attention to behavioral engagement. However, every day requires just the right amount of attention to cognitive engagement. Students only remember what they think about (Willingham, 2009), meaning that using strategies and learning activities that encourage students to think about the concepts they must master is a must.

So what types of learning environments or characteristics of learning environments promote a balanced environment with regard to student engagement? An environment that promotes all three types of engagement should (Almarode and Miller, 2013):

- Provide opportunities for students to explicitly identify and activate prior knowledge.

- Encourage students to explicitly link their prior knowledge to new learning.

- Engage students in activities that build background knowledge.

- Use novel experiences that capture the students' attention and excite them about ideas, concepts, and topics.

- Incorporate movement to evoke positive, emotionally charged events.

- Use strategies that are behaviorally relevant to the student such as essential questions, student choice, engaging scenarios, and inconsequential competition.

- Encourage students to ask questions, make mistakes, and respond to feedback.

- Enable students to see the big picture.

- Monitor the pace of instruction by providing students with opportunities to stop, process, and reflect on their learning.

- Include continual checks for understanding that encourage students to recall and review content.

Although a thorough examination of all of these characteristics is beyond the scope of this chapter, a closer look at identifying and activating prior knowledge as well as the pace of instruction will provide a starting point for how these characteristics support a balanced approach to student engagement.

IDENTIFYING AND ACTIVATING PRIOR KNOWLEDGE

When students walk into a classroom, their decision about whether to engage in the day's content and material often hinges on their perception of whether or not they can "get it" (Marzano, Pickering, and Heflebower, 2010). By ensuring that we provide opportunities for students to explicitly identify and activate their prior knowledge, we offer them an opportunity to dig up their own background knowledge and a greater chance that they will not only feel that they can get it but that they actually will get it. Identifying and activating prior knowledge helps the brain work smarter, not harder. Research suggests that when students explicitly engage in the activation of prior knowledge, they demonstrate improved encoding, retention, and recall (Alexander, Kulikowich, and Schulze, 1994; DeWitt, Knight, Hicks, and Ball, 2012; Schneider, 1993; Tobias, 1994).

Some examples of strategies that encourage students to identify and activate prior knowledge include:

> **Brainstorming or Word Splash**—Have students use notes from the previous class or a section of the text to create a list of key words, concepts, or phrases that they believe are important.
>
> **Concept Maps, Knowledge Maps, or Mind Maps**—Have students create a mind map of previous material. The key element of this strategy is that students must develop a sentence or phrase that justifies why two or more words, concepts, or phrases are linked together on the mind map.

Talk It Out—For each of the previous two strategies, have students pair up and talk about their word splashes or concept maps. One of the most effective ways to move something from short-term memory to long-term memory is to tell someone what you know (Medina, 2008).

Think-Puzzle-Explore—Provide students with a concept or idea from a previous class. Give them time to jot down whatever they *think* they know about the concept or idea. After some time, allow students to share what they think with a neighbor or as a class. Then provide them with time to make a list of things that puzzle them about the concept or idea. Again, allow students to share what they think with a neighbor or as a class. Finally, have students develop a list of questions about the idea or concept. These questions are the basis for identifying self-perceived gaps in knowledge (Ritchhart, Church, and Morrison, 2011).

MONITORING THE PACE OF INSTRUCTION

When it comes to the pace of instruction, the "Goldilocks principle" is a good rule of thumb. If the pace of instruction is too fast, students will disengage emotionally, behaviorally, and cognitively. Similarly, if the pace of instruction is too slow, students will disengage. The pace of instruction must be just right. What is just right? The student brain can focus for about 10 to 12 minutes on the content and material most commonly found in a classroom (Baddeley,

1999; Cowan, 2001). Although this may fluctuate with age, learner background knowledge, and complexity of the content (Jensen, 2005), the 10-to-12-minute rule is a reliable bet with the human brain. This limitation is linked to specific physiological characteristics of the brain (Baddeley, 1999; Cowan, 2001; Jensen, 2005). This reliable and natural feature of the human brain does not mean that we should teach for 10 or 12 minutes and then stop. Instead, we should break up instructional time into 10- to 12-minute chunks to provide students with opportunities to stop, process, and reflect on their learning throughout the class.

Some examples of strategies that monitor the pace of instruction and break up content into manageable chunks include:

Press and Release—Describes the general approach to monitoring the pace of instruction. As teachers, we should break the day or class period down into 10- to 12-minute segments. Between each segment, allow students to stop, process, and reflect (e.g., talk it out, writing exercise, word splash, mind map).

Discussion Circles—This cooperative learning strategy assigns specific roles (e.g., summarizer, mind mapper, vocabulary wizard, highlighter) and tasks to a specific chunk of content. Once students complete their specific role or task, they teach or share with their cooperative learning group.

Choice Boards—Students are given a menu of tasks associated with a specific topic. Examples of tasks include developing a set of worked examples in mathematics and teaching them to the class, developing a brochure about the Federal Court System, making and narrating a video of a science phenomenon, or recording a read-aloud. An adaptation to the choice board is to create enough tasks so that only two or three students can sign up for each one. Then students can work in small groups and the task becomes a cooperative learning activity.

Jigsaw—Students are assigned to an expert group, similar to the discussion circles groups, in which they develop expertise in a particular idea, concept, or topic. Each member understands that he or she will be responsible to share the knowledge he or she has gained with the larger group. For example, the teacher might develop expert groups on each application of the derivative in calculus (related rates, mean value, critical points, graphing, maximization and minimization problems, and differential equations). After an allotted amount of time, students return to their base groups and teach the material to the other members of the base group (Almarode and Miller, 2013).

CLASSROOM APPLICATION

Let's revisit the scenarios from above and see how the teachers could increase engagement for their students. For Mrs. Smith, starting class by activating prior knowledge will help students generate the cognitive power needed for the day's lesson. For example, Mrs. Smith could have students work in pairs and talk through the warm-up problems (talk it out), offering each other feedback on how they approached each problem or question. During the lesson, Mrs. Smith might consider breaking the class into 10- to 12-minute chunks by working a problem, then have students teach a similar problem to their neighbor. Digging up and activating prior knowledge as well as monitoring the pace of instruction will improve the cognitive and emotional engagement of her students.

For Mr. Jones, providing opportunities for students to explicitly process the information presented in documentaries, movies, and games will engage students cognitively and help them identify the key concepts from these activities. For example, Mr. Jones could use a word splash or concept map to activate and identify what his students recall from the readings about the Kennedy assassination. Following the documentary on this national tragedy, Mr. Jones could implement a discussion circle that encourages his students to think and talk about the content of the documentary as it relates to the content of his course (e.g., how the assassination was presented in the documentary versus the textbook, historical accuracies and inaccuracies, making inferences and drawing conclusions, the national impact of the event, remaining questions).

Mrs. Taylor's students would benefit from opportunities to cognitively process the large amount of information presented each day. Rather than taking a teacher-centered approach to content, Mrs. Taylor could emotionally, behaviorally, and cognitively engage her students by using strategies that encourage students to wrap their minds around the content. Word splashes, think-puzzle-explore activities, choice boards, and jigsaws would provide her students with the opportunity to recall prior learning (word splash) and take ownership of their learning (think-puzzle-explore, choice boards, and jigsaws) while monitoring the pace of instruction.

ENGAGED STUDENTS
STAY IN SCHOOL

It is all about engagement. As district administrators, building principals, and classroom teachers, we encounter factors that have a strong association with students' decision to stay in school or drop out. Many of these factors are beyond the teachers' control (minority status, poverty, family disruptions) and we cannot do anything to change these factors. However, research has continued to suggest that one very important factor associated with a student's decision to stay in school is engagement. This is a factor over which we have a lot of control. As teachers, we make decisions each day, hour, and minute in our classrooms that influence the level of student engagement. Ensuring that we foster and nurture an educational environment that emotionally, behaviorally, and cognitively engages our students makes the most of the small portion of time students spend in our classrooms. If we want to address the dropout problem, we have to start with engagement. If we want to engage students, we have to include their emotions, their behaviors, and their brains.

References

Abel, T., & Lattal, K. M. (2001). Molecular mechanisms of memory acquisition, consolidation and retrieval. *Current Opinion in Neurobiology, 11,* 180–187.

Alexander, P. A., Kulikowich, J. M., & Schulze, S. K. (1994). How subject-matter knowledge affects recall and interest. *American Educational Research Journal, 31*(2), 313–337.

Allensworth, E., & Easton, J. (2005). *The on-track indicator as a predictor of high school graduation.* Chicago, IL: Consortium for Chicago School Research.

Alliance for Excellent Education. (2009). *The high cost of high school dropouts: What the nation pays for inadequate high schools.* Washington, DC: Author. Retrieved from http://www.all4ed.org/about_the_crisis/impact/economic_analysis/

Almarode, J., & Miller, A. M. (2013). *Captivate, activate, and invigorate the student brain in science and math, grades 6–12.* Thousand Oaks, CA: Corwin Press.

Appleton, J., Christenson, S., & Furlong, M. (2008). Student engagement with school: Critical conceptual and methodological issues of the construct. *Psychology in the Schools, 45,* 369–386.

Baddeley, A. (1999). *Essentials of human memory.* Philadelphia, PA: Psychology Press.

Balfanz, R., & Legters, N. (2004). Locating the dropout crisis: Which high schools produce the nation's dropouts? In G. Orfield (Ed.), *Dropouts in America* (pp. 57–84). Cambridge, MA: Harvard Education Press.

Balfanz, R., & Neild, R. (2007). *Unfulfilled promise: The dimensions and characteristics of Philadelphia's dropout crisis, 2000–2005.* Philadelphia, PA: Project U-Turn.

Bliss, T. V. P., & Collingridge, G. L. (1993). A synaptic model of memory: Long-term potentiation in the hippocampus. *Nature, 361,* 31–39.

Bridgeland, J. M., DiIulio, J. J., & Morison, K. B. (2006). *The silent epidemic: Perspectives of high school dropouts.* Report by Civic Enterprises.

Christenson, S. L., Sinclair, M. F., Lehr, C. A., & Godber, Y. (2001). Promoting successful school completion: Critical conceptual and methodological guidelines. *School Psychology Quarterly, 16*(4), 468–484.

Cowan, N. (2001). The magical number 4 in short-term memory: A reconsideration of mental storage capacity. *Behavioral and Brain Sciences, 24,* 87–185.

DeWitt, M. R., Knight, J. B., Hicks, J. L., & Ball, B. H. (2012). The effects of prior knowledge on the encoding of episodic contextual details. *Psychonometric Bulletin Review, 19,* 251–257.

Fredricks, J. A., Blumenfeld, P. C., & Paris, A. H. (2004). School engagement: Potential of the concept, state of the evidence. *Review of Educational Research, 74*(1), 49–109.

Gleason, P., & Dynarski, M. (2002, January). Do we know whom to serve? Issues in using risk factors to identify dropouts. *Journal of Education on Students Placed at Risk, 1*(7), 25–41.

Jensen, E. (2005). *Teaching with the brain in mind* (2nd ed.). Alexandria, VA: Association for Supervision and Curriculum Development.

Jensen, E. (2009). *Teaching with poverty in mind: What being poor does to kids' brains and what schools can do about it.* Alexandria, VA: Association for Supervision and Curriculum Development.

Jerald, C. (2006). *Dropping out is hard to do.* Washington, DC: The Center for Comprehensive School Reform and Improvement.

Kandel, E. R. (1997). Genes, synapses, and long-term memory. *Journal of Cell Physiology, 173,* 124–125.

Levin, H., Belfield, C., Muennig, P., & Rouse, C. (2007, January). *The costs and benefits of an excellent education for all America's children.* New York: Center for Benefit-Cost Studies of Education at Columbia University, Teachers College, Columbia University. Retrieved from http://www.cbcse.org/media/download_gallery/Leeds_Report_Final_Jan2007.pdf

Marzano, R. J., Pickering, D. J., & Heflebower, T. (2010). *The highly engaged classroom.* Bloomington, IN: Solution Tree.

Medina, J. (2008). *Brain rules: 12 principles for surviving and thriving at work, home, and school.* Seattle, WA: Pear Press.

Miller, G. A. (1956). The magical number seven, plus or minus two: Some limits on our capacity for processing information. *Psychological Review, 63,* 81–97.

National Center for Education Statistics. (2012). *The condition of education. Status dropout rates (Indicator 33-2012).* Washington, DC: Institute of Education Sciences.

Nilsson, A., Radeborg, K., & Björck, I. (2012). Effects on cognitive performance of modulating the postprandial blood glucose profile at breakfast. *European Journal of Clinical Nutrition, 66,* 1039–1043.

Reschly, A., Huebner, E., Appleton, J., & Antaramian, S. (2008). Engagement as flourishing: The contribution of positive emotions and coping to adolescents' engagement at school and with learning. *Psychology in the Schools, 45,* 419–431.

Ritchhart, R., Church, M., & Morrison, K. (2011). *Making thinking visible: How to promote engagement, understanding, and independence for all learners.* San Francisco, CA: Jossey-Bass.

Roderick, M., & Camburn, E. (1999). Risk and recovery from course failure in the early years of high school. *American Educational Research Journal, 36,* 303–343.

Rouse, C. (2005, October). *The labor market consequences of an inadequate education.* Paper presented at the symposium on the social costs of inadequate education, Teachers College, Columbia University, New York.

Rumberger, R. W. (1995). Dropping out of middle school: A multilevel analysis of students and schools. *American Educational Research Journal, 32*(3), 583–625.

Rumberger, R. W. (2004). Why students drop out. In G. Orfield (Ed.), *Dropouts in America: Confronting the graduation rate crisis* (pp. 131–156). Cambridge, MA: Harvard Education Press.

Schneider, W. (1993). Domain-specific knowledge and memory performance in children. *Educational Psychology Review, 5,* 257–273.

Silva, A. J. (2003). Molecular and cellular cognitive studies of the role of synaptic plasticity in memory. *Journal of Neurobiology, 54,* 224–237.

Skinner, E., Kinderman, T., & Furrer, C. (2009). A motivational perspective on engagement and disaffection: Conceptualization and assessment of children's behavioral and emotional participation in academic activities in the classroom. *Educational and Psychological Measurement, 69,* 493–525.

Smith, K. A. (2000). Going deeper: Formal small-group learning in large classes. *New Directions for Teaching and Learning, 81,* 25–46.

Smith, M. A., & Foster, J. K. (2008). Glucoregulatory and order effects on verbal episodic memory in healthy adolescents after oral glucose administration. *Biological Psychology, 79,* 209–215.

Squire, L. R. (1992). Memory and the hippocampus: A synthesis from findings with rats, monkeys, and humans. *Psychological Review, 99*(2), 195–231.

Squire, L. R., & Cave, C. B. (1991). The hippocampus, memory, and space. *Hippocampus, 1*(3), 269–271.

Tobias, S. (1994). Interest, prior knowledge, and learning. *Review of Educational Research, 63,* 37–54.

Willingham, D. T. (2009). *Why don't students like school? A cognitive scientist answers questions about how the mind works and what it means for the classroom.* San Francisco, CA: Jossey-Bass.

Yazzie-Mintz, E. (2010). *Charting the path from engagement to achievement: A report on the 2009 high school survey of student engagement.* Bloomington, IN: Center for Evaluation & Education Policy.

CHAPTER FOUR

Instructional Leadership:

Leading Implementation of the Common Core

Stephen Ventura

There is growing research indicating that instructional leadership can result in a variety of educational improvements. But what do most school- and district-level leaders spend a majority of their time monitoring? I can remember being taught the "four Bs" of administration: buses, bonds, buildings, and budgets. It wasn't very long ago that these dominated the attention of most educational leaders. A majority of time was spent on maintaining or improving management functions. Even today, it is easy to conclude that many leaders spend most of their time on noninstructional or noneducational issues. Studying effective schools reveals one constant, no matter the organization: The most powerful variable in school improvement is strong instructional leadership.

Research conducted by King (2002), Elmore (2000), and Spillane, Halverson, and Diamond (2000) confirms that this important role extends beyond the scope of the school principal to involve other leaders as well. The key players in instructional leadership include the following:

- Central office personnel (superintendent, curriculum coordinators, etc.)
- Principals and assistant principals
- Instructional coaches

RETHINKING THE LEADERSHIP-MANAGEMENT DICHOTOMY

Think about your current role as a leader. How are you currently leading? One way to discern the differences between managers and leaders is to think of multiple ways to complete the following sentence: Managers do *this* _____, but leaders do *this* _____.

There are stark differences between the two. Managers concentrate on traditional leadership duties. These typically include methods of operations focused on site management. To be sure, these tasks are important; however, many managers have not learned to encompass the teaching-learning process.

Educational leaders are transformative by nature. In addition to understanding the relationship between standards and assessment, they also aim to inspire their people with a vision that energizes and encourages others to work collaboratively toward a common goal. That said, current school leadership is still fraught with managerial leaders who maintain 20th-century regimented school systems and carry on traditions that have been in place for generations.

Put simply, school managers measure their success by how the day went. They avoid conflict and prefer style over substance. School leaders focus on establishing goals, ensuring quality teaching, and provide for teacher learning and development. While leaders cannot ignore management duties, teaching and learning should be the area where most of the leaders' scheduled time is allocated.

To effectively implement the Common Core, leaders must have a balance of technical and adaptive leadership. Technical leadership focuses on problem solving or changes within the existing framework. Because many of these problems have a known solution, they can typically be solved by the building principal or other district experts. For example, the Common Core requires that literacy be a shared responsibility across all content areas with greater emphasis on nonfiction writing. Many schools and districts have required that all teachers, regardless of content, include more writing and informational text in their lessons.

Adaptive leadership is quite different. It involves deeper changes that ultimately alter existing values and norms. Solutions are not inherently evident until the leader establishes instructional norms in order for people to work together to find new solutions that will succeed. Goal setting, quality teaching, and teacher development are all examples of adaptive leadership. They provide meaningful opportunities for teachers to improve their professional practice.

KEY ELEMENTS OF INSTRUCTIONAL LEADERSHIP

In order to truly reap the benefits of instructional leadership, it is imperative to understand four simple elements of instructional alignment:

- Prioritization
- Research-based instructional strategies
- Focused and purposeful curriculum design and alignment
- Data analysis

Prioritization

What would you do if there were too many failures, too many discipline problems, and insufficient attendance at your school? Please select the most reasonable response.

a) Fire the principal

b) Fire the teachers

c) Get new students

d) Get a grant and buy 10 new programs and implement them simultaneously

e) Identify *one* or *two* high-leverage instructional practices and monitor implementation and results every week

I often have to remind clients that there is no research that states that frantic coverage of everything leads to better results. In fact, research supports the exact opposite—more focus and less coverage enables students and teachers to experience higher levels of success and student cognition. Moreover, instructional leaders understand that it is not the number of programs you implement, but the degree of implementation that makes a meaningful difference. Quality instruction does not equate to mountains of written plans and complex expectations. Quality instruction features an intense focus on those strategies that will have the greatest impact on student achievement.

Research-Based Instructional Strategies

It's important to begin with the definition of an instructional strategy: Instructional strategies are the actions of the teacher that are intended to lift the cognition of students in relation to specific learning goals. They are the methods by which the teacher increases student learning (Peery, 2009).

Put another way, a strategy is something an adult does; an activity is something a student does. Instructional leaders must be well informed about effective teaching strategies, especially since leaders will assist in supporting those strategies through implementation and monitoring. Effective schools agree on everyone learning some specific effective practices that are implemented, monitored, and used for feedback.

I have observed teacher frustration when it comes to strategy selection, because many teachers prefer teaching their favorite activities rather than the strategies students actually need. In these instances, instructional leaders can help teachers create selection criteria for instructional strategies. Have teachers discuss these criteria as they begin to select strategies that have been determined to meet the specific needs of learners. To get the selection process started, teachers could, for example, decide that if the strategy a teacher suggests meets at least four of the agreed-upon criteria, the strategy can be implemented. However, if the strategy meets three or fewer, they must adjust that strategy until it meets more selection criteria. A list of possible selection criteria might include:

- Directly targets the prioritized needs of students, especially when analyzing formative assessments scores.
- Modifies teachers' instructional practice.
- Describes actions of the adults that change the thinking of the students.
- Includes scaffolding methods suitable for each performance group of students.
- Was agreed upon by the team tó be one of the no more than three prioritized research-based strategies that will have the greatest impact.
- Is described specifically enough to allow for replication (the implementation, frequency, duration, and resources are all described thoroughly).

Focused and Purposeful Curriculum Design and Alignment

If student achievement is the goal and that goal is measured by standards-based assessments, then there must be a comprehensive framework that intentionally aligns standards, assessments, instruction, curriculum, and data analysis within each unit of study. One of the best collaborative strategies teachers can use is to prioritize the Common Core standards. The focus on prioritized standards is on learning, not mere coverage. And, prioritizing the standards does not equate to elimination. The process gives every student in the district an opportunity to learn what is most essential.

Priority Standards, also called Power Standards (Ainsworth, 2003), are a carefully selected subset of all standards. These are the standards students *must* know and be able to do by the end of the school year. In addition to providing focus for units of study, they also serve as the standards that common formative assessments are made up of.

Instructional leaders realize the power of focus. Here are two critical questions to consider (Ainsworth, 2010):

- Are all of the Common Core State Standards at the elementary, middle, and high school levels essential for students to acquire in order to be ready for the standards at the next level of learning?

- Will the length of the school year afford teachers the time needed to adequately teach, assess, reteach, and reassess students on all of the standards?

Perfect coverage of any curriculum is an illusion, but many state education departments have stated that the CCSS cannot be "powered." In other words, their position is that there are fewer standards in the CCSS documents than in many standards systems, and all of them are essential and deserve the same amount of instructional focus. Even if we accept that the CCSS are adequately focused, enabling teachers to cover all of them without any prioritization, the assumption is that students need to gain only one year of learning to achieve those standards. But in my experience as a professional developer, many of the schools I serve have students who need more than one year of learning to achieve proficiency. And if the CCSS are more rigorous than previously established state standards, then even more students will need more than one year of learning in order to achieve grade-level proficiency (Reeves, et al., 2011).

Helping teachers understand that some standards are more important than others gives instructional leaders credibility, especially if you are working in an environment where "everything is important."

Data Analysis

In their focus on improving achievement, effective leaders use multiple sources of information to assess performance (National Association of Elementary School Principals, 2001). Decisions at all levels must be based on pertinent data. Central office staff can use data to help principals become more effective instructional leaders and to make decisions regarding policy and curriculum. Principals can use data to help guide the instructional focus and professional development of teachers. Coaches can use data to determine the effectiveness of instructional strategies. Coaches can also assist teachers in using data to establish student grouping arrangements and to pinpoint specific student intervention needs.

One of the best ways to determine how to improve the use of data in your school is to conduct an assessment of where your organization currently is with respect to data analysis. The goal of the self-assessment is to identify your organization's present use of data and then decide where you would like to be. Have stakeholders read each level of data analysis (descriptions follow), underlining and highlighting specific phrases that resonate with them. After reading all five levels, team members should discuss current and future uses of data. If your team is like the thousands of educators who have participated in this activity, they will gravitate towards level 3—data application. The goal is to move an organization to level 4—data mastery. Level 5—data inspiration—can only be attained by demonstrating solid level 4 analysis.

Level 1—Data Averseness: "The use of data is unfair and evaluative. If we look at data at the student level, we violate their privacy. If we look at data at the teacher level, we violate their professionalism. Worst of all, if we emphasize student data, we encourage poor teaching and cheating. Whatever benefits there may be, the risks are greater and data analysis is just not worth the effort."

Level 2—Data Awareness: "I'm willing to look at the data—perhaps at the school and district level. Sometimes it is interesting to see how students performed and how schools are different. But I can't say that data analysis influences teaching and leadership. We certainly do not measure teaching and leadership. In fact, I'm not sure that measuring those qualities is even possible."

Level 3—Data Application: "We look at a variety of sources of student data, including state, local, school, and classroom-based assessments. We also look at teaching and leadership strategies, such as the time we allocate to various subjects and the frequency of feedback we provide to students. We regularly compare causes—teaching and leadership—with effects—student performance, and we have evidence that we adjust practices accordingly."

Level 4—Data Mastery: "We regularly use data to challenge our assumptions about teaching, leadership, and learning. We can think of specific changes we've made and mistakes we've made, and we can also think of specific instances in which we have affirmed our best practices, even if they were not very popular. Most importantly, we can identify how we have used our best practices to assist our colleagues in other schools and other systems. We use data not just to be more professional, but to improve the world of education."

Level 5—Data Inspiration: "Our students use data to provide self-assessment and immediate feedback and we have specific, compelling, and inspirational examples in which students challenge themselves to ever-higher levels of performance far beyond what traditional standards and testing would have accomplished."

There are three tips instructional leaders should consider as they navigate and prioritize student performance results.

First, instructional leaders must commit to data analysis as a continuous process. A study by the Bay Area School Reform Collaborative (Oberman and Symonds, 2005) demonstrates that schools that reviewed data several times each month were far more likely to close achievement gaps than those that reviewed data only a few times a year.

Second, start with a clearly focused question, such as: What are our greatest areas of strength in writing for our eighth-grade students? Which specific math skills are weakest in fifth grade? Why are we experiencing the same test scores, with different students, year after year?

Third, go beyond just numbers to consider what actually causes student success and failure. When we only study student demographic characteristics, we tend to assume that the causes of high or low achievement are related to family income, ethnicity, gender, and primary language. This type of limited analysis avoids a consideration of the powerful influences of teaching practices, curriculum, and feedback, just to name a few variables you won't find in a data warehouse. It's easy to create PowerPoint slides and wall charts showing demographic data. It's more challenging—but more important—to have discussions about how adult teaching and leadership behaviors can improve student achievement.

Many schools and districts have implemented collaboration time for teachers and leaders to discuss and analyze data. The Data Teams structure is an efficient system to continuously and collaboratively analyze student performance in order to refocus teaching strategies to impact student learning throughout the school year. By using Data Teams to select appropriate instructional strategies, instructional leaders can expect tremendous results. The Data Teams process is also inextricably linked to Response to Intervention and differentiated instruction, which provides improved performance in a structured manner (Reeves, 2009).

Following the steps of the Data Teams process can help your school and organization reach data mastery—a solid level 4 of data analysis.

TOP FIVE LEADERSHIP ACTIONS FOR COMMON CORE SUCCESS

As schools and districts transition to the Common Core, there are specific behaviors and actions that can help organizations become ready for implementation. Here are five specific leadership strategies that will prepare your school and district for Common Core success:

1. Ensure teachers are familiar with the instructional shifts needed for the Common Core. There are six instructional shifts that need to be made in order to effectively implement the Common Core State Standards in English language arts and literacy, and six shifts to implement them in math (EngageNY, n.d.). Teachers must understand that these shifts not only affect their current instruction, but also are reflected in assessments. To be truly aligned with Common Core implementation, these twelve shifts are non-negotiable. For a complete copy of all twelve shifts, please visit www.engageny.org.

2. Have teachers examine the anchor standards and K–12 standards in ELA and the learning progressions K–8 in math, regardless of the grade level they teach.

3. Provide time for teachers to deconstruct, or "unwrap," their standards, with an emphasis on cognition levels (Bloom's taxonomy and Webb's Depth of Knowledge) and how their grade-specific standards impact the success of students at all grades.

4. Align classroom instruction and formative assessments to the rigor of the Common Core standards and the cognition levels of next generation assessments, such as those developed by PARCC (Partnership for Assessment of Readiness for College and Careers) or the Smarter Balanced Assessment Consortium.

5. Develop a coherent grade-by-grade curriculum based on college- and career-readiness characteristics, with rich units of study that cluster standards around challenging performance tasks similar to those on PARCC and Smarter Balanced assessments.

STUDENT RESPONSIBILITY FOR LEARNING— MOVE THEM TO MATURITY

Many teachers become frustrated with students because of their lack of enthusiasm for content, low levels of engagement and homework completion, and increases in student failure. Leaders must help teachers understand that they are not teaching full-grown adults with adult-level competencies. They are teaching young humans who are learning those competencies for the first time. This does not mean we "go easy" on students. In fact, we need to teach them to take greater responsibility for their own learning, and this should start on the first day of school.

The next time you conduct a classroom walkthrough, pay attention to the classroom routine. In most classrooms I have observed, students enter the room and wait for the teacher to tell them what to do; or they follow a "get started" activity written on the board that the teacher created. In this type of environment, the teacher—not the student—is responsible for most of the learning.

How much more enjoyable would teaching be if teachers had classrooms where students walk through the door and immediately understand the difference between their social world (outside the classroom) and the world of work (inside the classroom)? Students pick up a portfolio folder, or log onto a Web site that features their current work and a specific schedule that students developed the prior day; they read through comments from the teacher that include specific feedback on how to improve their performance; and then they start working on activities they choose. Students determine what materials they'll need to complete their tasks, and they sign up for those activities, including small-group mini-lessons taught by the teacher. They use rubrics and scoring guides to gauge their work and understand how to assess their own progress; and they are able to tell the teacher how well they are doing and what the teacher can do to help them be more successful. The teacher has now created an environment that has been carefully structured so that students take more responsibility for their own learning. Student responsibility for learning requires clear expectations, structures that students use to achieve success, and guidance and feedback from the teacher. The methods in Jim Knight's *High-Impact Instruction* (2013) can help make this vision a reality.

ACADEMIC RIGOR

When students are engaged in learning and are taught to take greater responsibility for their own learning, then increasing academic rigor is attainable. Antiquated teaching strategies such as lecturing, drilling, and rote memorization will not increase learning. These strategies may lead to small, short-term increases in high-stakes assessments, but as time goes by, the students will have little to show for their work, and little foundation to build upon the following year. If you engage students' minds in grappling with content through meaningful, authentic performance tasks, they will build knowledge and understanding for the long term. If you increase their responsibility for learning, offering them freedom and choice, they will be able to accomplish more, not remaining dependent on others to continue moving forward. You can then increase academic rigor through well-designed assignments, questions, differentiation, collaboration, and a host of other meaningful learning opportunities.

LEADING TOWARD SUCCESS

Instructional leadership does not have to be a source of stress and fatigue. In fact, with the right conditions, it is not necessary to micromanage every function of instruction. Specific leadership actions are directly related to student achievement. It is clear that what leaders do to create a better environment for teachers and for student learning has a clear, measurable and profound impact on student learning. Focusing on leadership rather than management values, monitoring adult teaching practices, and maintaining a laser-like focus on fewer initiatives remain remarkably constant predictors of success according to the research, even as researchers change.

As more leaders adjust their roles to reflect a focus on instructional improvements that will directly influence student achievement, the process of systemic improvements necessary for lasting positive change in education will continue to gain momentum.

References

Ainsworth, L. (2003). *Power standards: Identifying the standards that matter the most.* Englewood, CO: Advanced Learning Press.

Ainsworth, L. (2010). *Rigorous curriculum design: How to create curricular units of study that align standards, instruction, and assessment.* Englewood, CO: Lead + Learn Press.

Elmore, R. (2000). *Building a new structure for school leadership.* Washington, DC: The Albert Shanker Institute.

EngageNY. (n.d.). Pedagogical shifts demanded by the common core state standards. Retrieved from http://www.engageny.org./sites/default/files/resource/attachments/common-core-shifts.pdf

King, D. (2002). The changing shape of leadership. *Educational Leadership, 59*(8), 61–63.

Knight, J. (2013). *High-impact instruction: A framework for great teaching.* Thousand Oaks, CA: Corwin.

National Association of Elementary School Principals. (2001). *Leading learning communities: Standards for what principals should know and be able to do.* Alexandria, VA: Author.

Oberman, I., & Symonds, K. W. (2005). What matters most in closing the gap. *Leadership, 34*(3), 8–11.

Peery, A. (2009). *Power strategies for effective teaching.* Englewood, CO: Lead + Learn Press.

Reeves, D. B. (2009). Looking deeper into the data. *Educational Leadership, 66*(4), 89–90.

Reeves, D. B., Wiggs, M. D., Lassiter, C. J., Piercy, T. D., Ventura, S., & Bell, B. (2011). *Navigating implementation of the common core state standards.* Englewood, CO: Lead + Learn Press.

Spillane, J. P., Halverson, R., & Diamond, J. B. (2000). *Toward a theory of leadership practice: A distributed perspective.* Evanston, IL: Institute for Policy Research.

CHAPTER FIVE

Five to Thrive:
Strategies that Promote Learning

Lissa Pijanowski

"Instruction should not be a Ouija board–like game in which teachers guess about what to do next. Educating kids is far too important for that sort of approach."

W. J. POPHAM, 2008, p.14

While reviewing the February 2012 issue of *Education Week*, an article title caught my attention—"Common Standards Will Not Affect Student Achievement" (Gewertz, 2012). Of course, this compelled me to read further, considering the historical national movement toward the new standards. The assertions, outlined in The 2012 Brown Center Report on American Education (Loveless, 2012), were correct. Standards will not improve achievement ... instruction will. Whether it is the Common Core or another set of academic standards, learning is accelerated by the instruction provided by the teacher, and not by the standards alone. The evidence is compelling. In the 1970s, The International Association for the Evaluation of Educational Achievement (IEA) coined the term "opportunity to learn," asserting that there are three types of curriculum—intended, implemented, and achieved (Loveless, 2012). The "intended" curriculum refers to the standards themselves, in this case the Common Core. The "implemented" curriculum is what teachers teach—it is the instruction provided to students. Finally, there is the "achieved" curriculum, which reflects what the students actually learn. Where we need to expend our energy is on the implemented curriculum, to ensure that all teachers have the tools they need to provide high-quality, research-based instruction aligned with the well-intended CCSS.

So, do you think all teachers have the right tools for the job? I would argue that teachers typically have a few great strategies in their toolbox that they use regularly. Then, they have a few more strategies that they have tried or that they recognize. It is imperative that we fill the classroom teacher's toolbox with a variety of strategies that will help their students thrive in a rigorous, relevant learning environment. Therefore, I believe there are five strategic areas that deserve our attention. I call them the "five to thrive":

- Activation
- Collaboration
- Metacognition
- Communication
- Application

Within each of these five categories teachers will find research-based instructional strategies to better meet the demands of the Common Core, as well as the next generation assessments from the Partnership for Assessment of Readiness for College and Careers (PARCC) and the Smarter Balanced Assessment Consortium (SBAC), slated for implementation in 2014/15.

ACTIVATION

Activating a student's knowledge is a key factor for both increasing student engagement and building a context for learning. From the time a lesson is introduced, students make a decision about the effort they will put forth to learn. Some decisions are based on their level of interest in the content; however, some decisions are based on a lack of background knowledge or a lack of understanding about the relevance of the subject to their lives. Have you ever heard the following questions: Why do I need to know this? How is this going to help me get into college? I don't know—what does it mean?

The following activation strategies provide teachers with options for setting a context for learning from the onset of a lesson. By activating prior knowledge, teachers set their students up for success. Dr. Madeline Hunter, author of the seven-step lesson design model (1994), called this the "anticipatory set" and referred to these strategies as "hooks" to build student interest and knowledge. (Additional explanation is offered about strategies marked with an asterisk.)

- Academic vocabulary
- Background knowledge
- Essential questions
- Advance organizers, including anticipation guides*
- K-W-L (know-wonder-learn)
- Teacher- and student-generated comparisons
- Student learning goals*
- Preview content

Advance organizers assist students with accessing prior knowledge in preparation for new learning. There are four formats for organizers—expository, narrative, skimming, and graphic.

- Anticipation guides are an example of an expository advance organizer and emphasize the essential learning. This can take the form of a content statement, asking students to agree or disagree, and then after experiencing the reading, video, or lesson students would confirm or revise their initial response.

- Narrative advance organizers refer to setting up a learning experience through reading an excerpt from an article or story, showing a video clip, introducing key vocabulary, or even sharing a personal story. This strategy engages students' interest and sets the stage for learning.

- Skimming the text with purpose can be a powerful tool. Teachers can model for students how to create a conceptual framework through skimming different types of text. Additionally, providing focus questions to guide students is beneficial: What can you predict from the title? What is the flow of the text (subheadings, amount of content)? What are the Big Ideas? What can the illustrations tell you about the text?

- Graphic advance organizers are used in advance of instruction and communicate learning expectations. Teachers can modify traditional organizer formats to fit the content.

Research in support of advance organizers includes *Visible Learning* (Hattie, 2009, p. 167), which show an effect size of 0.41;

and *Classroom Instruction that Works* (Dean, Hubbell, Pitler, and Stone, 2012, p. 57), which shows an effect size of 0.59 for combined cues, questions, and advance organizers.

Student learning goals inform performance expectations and promote students monitoring their own progress. Additionally, specific learning goals can elicit feedback that is timely and relevant. Encouraging students to write challenging yet attainable goals customized to meet their individual learning needs helps to engage learners and promotes a greater sense of self-efficacy. For students who struggle, the incremental goals make the work more palatable and often promote reinforcement of effort and recognition.

There are several recommendations for creating student learning goals (Dean, et al., 2012, p. 5):

- Set learning goals (objectives) that are specific but not restrictive.
- Communicate the learning goals (objectives) to students and parents.
- Connect learning goals (objectives) to previous and future learning.
- Engage students in setting personal learning goals (objectives).

Research in support of student learning goals includes *Visible Learning* (Hattie, 2009, pp. 163–164), which shows an effect size of 0.56; and *Classroom Instruction that Works* (Dean, et al., 2012, pp. 3–4), which shows an effect size of 0.61 for combined setting objectives and providing feedback.

COLLABORATION

Learning is a very social activity. We learn best when we engage with others, talk about ideas, and experience new concepts. For far too long, traditional education has emphasized a one-to-one relationship between student and content. In contrast, a more forward-thinking education should recognize the social aspect of learning as a tool to better prepare students for college and careers. As an outcome of the Common Core, working collaboratively should become commonplace in the modern classroom and be leveraged to help students construct meaning.

The following strategies offer opportunities to engage students in collaborative learning experiences. John Dewey (1916) rejected the notion that schools should focus on repetitive, rote memorization and proposed a method of "directed living"—students would engage in real-world, practical workshops in which they would demonstrate their knowledge through creativity and collaboration. Students should be provided with opportunities to think for themselves and articulate their thoughts on a daily basis. (Additional explanation is offered about strategies marked with an asterisk.)

- Cooperative learning*
- Reciprocal teaching*
- Jigsaw
- Socratic seminar
- Feedback—peer-to-peer/teacher-student
- Games for learning
- Simulation/role playing

Cooperative learning promotes interdependence, peer interaction, individual and group accountability, interpersonal skills, and group processing, such as problem solving. Additionally, cooperative learning provides structures for students to deepen and enhance their knowledge while satisfying their need to socially interact with others. Students are more able to collectively make and learn from errors, and their conversations can assist in having the goals, learning intentions, and success criteria spelled out for all (Hattie, 2009, p. 214).

Effective cooperative learning groups have the following characteristics (Dean, et al., 2012, p. 39):

- Include both positive interdependence and individual accountability
- Are small in size
- Are used consistently and systematically

Research in support of cooperative learning includes *Visible Learning* (Hattie, 2009, pp. 212–214), which shows an effect size of 0.59 for cooperative vs. individualistic learning; and *Classroom Instruction that Works* (Dean, et al., 2012, pp. 88–89), which shows an effect size of 1.00.

Reciprocal teaching is a reading technique that provides students with four different strategies that are actively and consciously used to support comprehension. The purpose of reciprocal teaching is to facilitate a group effort between teacher and students as well as among students in the task of bringing meaning to text (Palincsar, 1986). The most effective use of the strategy is as a small-group collaborative discussion where participants take turns assuming the role of the teacher. The four strategies of reciprocal teaching are outlined below.

- Questioning is where readers monitor and assess their own understanding by asking themselves questions related to the information, themes, and ideas represented in the text.

- Clarifying focuses on unclear, difficult, or unfamiliar aspects of the text and on using strategies such as decoding or context clues to better understand the text.

- Summarizing requires the reader to distinguish important ideas, themes, and information within a text and to create concise statements that communicate the main idea.

- Predicting integrates a reader's own prior knowledge with text structures to create a hypothesis related to the author's purpose.

Research in support of reciprocal teaching includes *Visible Learning* (Hattie, 2009, pp. 203–204), which shows an effect size of 0.74; and *Classroom Instruction that Works* (Dean, et al., 2012, pp. 88–89), which shows an effect size of 1.00 for combined summarizing and notetaking.

METACOGNITION

Teaching students explicitly how to think about their own thinking is an integral part of preparing students for more rigorous content and sets them up for academic success. Modeling for students how to organize their thoughts, plan an approach toward a task, make connections, understand relationships, and monitor their own progress are all part of learning. Research from *Visible Learning* (Hattie, 2009) reflects a 0.69 effect size for metacognitive strategies.

Students who demonstrate a wide range of metacognitive skills are self-regulated learners. Learners who take control of their own learning through evaluating and monitoring their progress and behaviors are more likely to achieve their learning goals.

Teachers need to empower students with metacognitive skills to address three kinds of content knowledge: declarative, procedural, and conditional (Metcalfe and Shimamura, 1994). Declarative knowledge is the factual information that one knows. Strategies for organizing information would assist students with this type of knowledge. Procedural knowledge is knowledge of how to do something—of how to perform the steps in a process (for example, knowing how to plan a performance task or research paper). Conditional knowledge is knowledge about when to use a procedure, skill, or strategy and when not to use it; why a procedure works and under what conditions; and why one procedure is better than another. For example, students having the ability to think through the strategies they need to employ to solve a multi-step word problem is a critical skill that falls into this category.

Below are examples of strategies that help students organize new learning and ideas, think through the learning process, and become more self-sufficient. (Additional explanation is offered about strategies marked with an asterisk.)

- Nonlinguistic representations*
- Concept mapping*
- Summarizing/notetaking
- Read/recall/check/summarize
- Content frames
- Interacting with text

- Similarities and differences
- Close read
- Annotations
- Think out loud
- Self-assessment

Nonlinguistic representations and **concept mapping** refer to graphic and pictorial representations of key concepts being studied. This strategy emphasizes the identification of major ideas, themes, and interrelationships in order to enhance reading comprehension and conceptual understanding. It is often very successful with helping struggling students organize and synthesize ideas. Concept mapping is most effective when done by the student and tends to increase engagement. The following are examples of nonlinguistic representations.

- Concept maps are where students create a word web, with the main idea in the center and key details on the outside. This can be used as a pre-reading, during-reading, and post-reading activity. Students add details to the map as they read and discuss.

- Free-form maps allow students to create their own representation of content through both pictures and words. This strategy is meant to be collaborative and taps into student creativity.

- Sequence maps can be used when there needs to be representation of a progression of events, and can be a combination of pictures and words.

- Character maps can be used to validate an opinion about a character or during reading to gather information about the character. They can include both pictures and text.

• Comparison maps, such as a Venn diagram, can be used to highlight similarities and differences among concepts, characters, and events.

Research in support of concept mapping includes *Visible Learning* (Hattie, 2009, pp. 168–169), which shows an effect size of 0.57; and *Classroom Instruction that Works* (Dean, et al., 2012, pp. 64–65), which shows an effect size of 0.75 in the original meta-analysis, and 0.49 in the updated 2010 McREL study (Beesley and Apthorp, 2010), equal to achievement gains of 19 percentile points for nonlinguistic representation.

COMMUNICATION

Teaching the language of learning is a strategy in and of itself. The Common Core emphasizes not only writing, but also speaking and listening. The opportunities provided for students to engage in speaking, listening, and writing are life skills and deserve classroom time and attention. Often oral presentations, meaningful class discussions, and writing are cast aside due to limited instructional time. Students need an authentic audience to motivate them to excel. We have all seen it happen time and time again. If students know they are going to present in front of peers and/or other adults, the effort and attention they give to the task increases significantly.

We also know that writing is not assigned as frequently as it should be due to the amount of time it takes to evaluate and provide feedback. But not all writing has to be an essay. Students can relay understanding through quick-writes or constructed responses. Students should be writing daily and in all subjects. Additionally, the use of benchmark papers, modeling, and scoring guides increases the likelihood that products will meet expectations. The Common Core requires that by twelfth grade 80 percent of student writing should be informational (explanatory) or argumentative (persuasive). The next generation assessments mirror these requirements in writing, with both short and extended constructed responses. Therefore, we must structure our courses of study to include meaningful writing opportunities and provide students with feedback.

Additionally, communication of learning expectations is a high-leverage strategy that should guide the focus of instruction and the actions of students. By utilizing strategies such as guided practice, modeling, and scoring guides, teachers can increase student understanding of the goals for learning and therefore produce higher results. Suggested communication strategies are listed below. (Additional explanation is offered about strategies marked with an asterisk.)

- Powerful questioning*
- QARs—question, answer, relationship
- RAFT—Role, audience, format, topic
- Writing to learn strategies
- Constructed response
- Argumentation*
- Benchmark work
- Anchor papers
- Learning targets
- Scoring guides and rubrics

- Guided practice
- Modeling

Powerful questioning refers to the teacher's role in engaging students in higher-order thinking through posing inferential or analytic questions (Dean, et al., 2012, pp. 54–57). Teachers ask an average of 100 questions per hour; however, on average, 60–70 percent of those questions require recall and another 20 percent are procedural in nature. Some tips for increasing the effectiveness of questioning are (Peery, 2009):

- Plan questions in advance and ask open-ended, thought-provoking questions that require students to analyze and make inferences about the content.

- Create assignments that require all students to answer questions, such as exit slips, think-pair-share, and interactive whiteboard clickers.

- Determine a system for involving a wide variety of students, not just those who volunteer.

A new publication from Lead + Learn Press, *Ask, Don't Tell: Powerful Questioning in the Classroom* (2013) by Angela Peery, Polly Patrick, and Deb Moore, provides detailed information about how to improve questioning in the classroom.

Research in support of questioning includes *Visible Learning* (Hattie, 2009, pp. 182–183), which shows an effect size of 0.46; and *Classroom Instruction that Works* (Dean, et al., 2012, pp. 51–57), which shows an effect size of 0.59 for combined cues, questions, and advance organizers, with an additional study (Dean, et al., 2012, p. 52) noted for an effect size of 1.18 for questioning and achievement in reading comprehension.

Argumentation is a strategy that can be used across disciplines and that embodies creating and communicating an argument. The process can include debate, dialogue, conversation, and persuasion, and above all, must be claims-based. Beginning in sixth grade, the Common Core requires proficient argumentation. The standards say students must "cite textual evidence to support analysis of what the text says explicitly as well as inferences drawn from the text" and "write arguments to support claims with clear reasons and relevant evidence." And one of the Common Core's mathematical practice standards states that students must be able to "construct viable arguments and critique the reasoning of others."

To create a viable argument, students must:

- Research a topic, problem, or situation.
- Create a minimum of two claims.
- Organize data/facts/textual evidence to support the claims.
- Provide a conclusion.

Arguments can be written or presented orally. This strategy represents a critical skill; as noted in Appendix A of the ELA Common Core State Standards, argumentative writing should represent 40 percent of a student's writing by grade 12, followed by 40 percent explanatory or informational writing, with only 20 percent for conveying experience, or narrative writing (National Governors Association Center for Best Practices and Council of Chief State School Officers, 2010). With so many applications for argumentation across disciplines, the possibilities are endless.

Research in support of writing programs includes *Visible Learning* (Hattie, 2009, pp. 141–143), which shows an effect size of

0.44. If students are explicitly taught strategies for planning, revising, and editing, the effect size is 0.82, particularly if they are struggling students. Strategies for summarizing reading materials have an effect size of 0.82 and strategies for setting clear and specific goals for what students are to accomplish with their writing product have an effect size of 0.70.

APPLICATION

Finally, asking students to apply their knowledge gives them the opportunity to show what they know. The shift from instruction of discrete standards to incorporating standards into engaging learning experiences is a welcome change. Balancing skills-based, direct instruction with time for students to construct their own knowledge is the focus of the application category of strategies. When teachers build performance tasks and project-based learning experiences, they show excitement about instruction and make statements such as, "I can't wait to teach this" or "This is the way I love to teach." I truly believe that structuring students' application of knowledge around authentic, real-world problems will pay huge dividends in terms of student learning. Likewise, those results will translate into a successful transition to the next generation assessments that will require performance tasks in both reading and mathematics.

Below are some examples of strategies that can be used to foster application of knowledge and skills and create rich learning experiences for students. (Additional explanation is offered about strategies marked with an asterisk.)

- Authentic performance tasks, or problem-based learning*

- Project-based learning
- Inquiry
- Individual contracts
- Generating/testing hypotheses*
- Portfolios
- Interactive notebooks

Authentic performance tasks, or problem-based learning activities, have the following characteristics (Gijbels, 2005):

- Learning is student-centered.
- Learning occurs individually and/or in small groups.
- The teacher serves as the facilitator or guide.
- Authentic problems, scenarios, or challenges are presented at the beginning of the unit of study.
- The tasks are designed to assist the student with achieving the required knowledge and skills necessary to solve the problem.
- New information is acquired through self-directed learning.

Creation of authentic, problem-based learning is a core component of the *Rigorous Curriculum Design* (Ainsworth, 2010) model that is being used across the nation to plan units of study for the Common Core. The integration of performance tasks throughout the unit allows for direct instruction, scaffolding learning, and authentic assessment prior to the end-of-unit assessment.

Visible Learning (Hattie, 2009, pp. 210–211) shows an effect size of 0.61 for problem-based learning.

Generating and testing hypotheses utilizes the thinking processes of deduction and inference making. These processes deepen student knowledge due to the use of critical thinking skills such as analysis and evaluation. The strategy is also very motivating for students, as it poses a problem to be solved—a puzzle. Students generate a hypothesis; for example: If (action), then (outcome). Then, students have to work to validate their answers. Four processes are outlined in *Classroom Instruction that Works* (Dean, et al., 2012):

- Systems analysis is the process of analyzing the parts of a system and the manner in which they interact (p. 139).

- Problem solving involves overcoming constraints or limiting conditions that are in the way of achieving goals (p. 140).

- Experimental inquiry is the process of generating and testing explanations of observed phenomena (p. 142).

- Investigation is the process of identifying and resolving issues regarding past events about which there are confusions or contradictions (p. 144).

Classroom Instruction that Works (Dean, et al., 2012, p. 137) shows an effect size of 0.61 for generating and testing hypotheses.

DATA TEAMS

Before choosing strategies, teachers must first seek to understand the needs of their students, so that they can choose the strategies with the greatest likelihood of helping students reach their learning goals. The Data Teams process outlines specific steps for teams of teachers to utilize to focus their conversation around the results of a common formative assessment:

1. Collect and chart data

2. Analyze data and prioritize needs

3. Set, review, and revise incremental SMART goals (specific, measurable, attainable, relevant, timely)

4. Select common instructional strategies

5. Determine results indicators

6. Monitor and evaluate results

There is an explicit connection between the analysis of student work and the selection of strategies. The process is very intentional and eliminates the guesswork in determining what will work with different groups of students. With the requirements of Response to Intervention (RTI) and the need to differentiate instruction, Data Teams help teachers collaboratively determine next steps for instruction. Students are organized into four different groups—students who are proficient, students who are close to proficient (Tier 1), students who have far to go (Tier 2), and students who need intense intervention (Tier 3). Teams select strategies appropriate for the needs of each group that are focused on the Priority Standard(s), or learning target(s). These steps, implemented with fidelity and in conjunction with monitoring and evaluation by leadership, result in dramatic gains in student achievement and greater efficacy on the part of teachers.

FIVE TO THRIVE FOR STUDENTS

With the ultimate goal being development of students who are self-regulated learners, providing the *"five to thrive"* in student-friendly language is beneficial. Students should come to understand teacher expectations and begin to employ various strategies without being prompted. Communicating the student version also aids teachers when modeling for students the use of the strategies and when they are most appropriate.

The student-friendly version of the "five to thrive" is:

1. Activate my knowledge.

2. Collaborate with others.

3. Think about my own thinking.

4. Communicate my learning.

5. Show what I know.

WHY FIVE?

The five categories were selected following an extensive review of the research on instruction, effective schools, and preparing students for the future. Just as students need a way to think about their own thinking, teachers need a way to think about their own teaching. The five categories of activation, collaboration, metacognition, communication, and application also represent an alignment with the performance expectations within the Common Core State Standards, the Next Generation Science Standards, and the next generation assessments from PARCC and SBAC. Additionally, the framework published by the Partnership for 21st Century Skills (n.d.) promotes the "four c's—collaboration, communication, critical thinking (metacognition), and creativity (application)—as necessary skills to prepare our students for college and careers. You will find evidence of these within the five categories as well.

Regardless of the standards and the assessments, the one thing that makes the biggest difference in student learning is the quality of instruction in the classroom. While there are many variables that contribute to a student's learning experience, it is the quality of instruction provided by the teacher that can be isolated as a means to dramatically improve student achievement. It's true: the Common Core will not improve student achievement ... instruction will. "Five to thrive" fills the teacher toolbox with high-leverage, research-based strategies. Additionally, it provides a framework for teachers to design learning experiences that are relevant and meaningful. For students, "five to thrive" provides opportunities to become independent, self-regulated learners. Learning is a process, and we must empower students to become better thinkers, collaborators, and creators to prepare them for the world in which we live. Let's bring back the joy of teaching and learning. Leverage the "five to thrive" to build rigorous and relevant classrooms where learning flourishes and both teachers and students experience success.

References

Ainsworth, L. (2010). *Rigorous curriculum design: How to create curricular units of study that align standards, instruction, and assessment.* Englewood, CO: Lead + Learn Press.

Beesley, A. D., & Apthorp, H. S. (2010). *Classroom instruction that works, second edition: Research report.* Denver, CO: Mid-continent Research for Education and Learning.

Dean, C., Hubbell, E., Pitler, H., & Stone, B. (2012). *Classroom instruction that works: Research-based strategies for increasing student achievement* (2nd ed.). Alexandria, VA: ASCD.

Dewey, J. (1916). *Democracy and education: An introduction to the philosophy of education.* New York, NY: Macmillan.

Gewertz, C. (2012). Common standards will not affect student achievement. *Education Week.* Retrieved from http://blogs.edweek.org/edweek/curriculum/2012/02/brookings_report_explores_comm.html

Gijbels, D. (2005). Effects of problem-based learning: A meta-analysis. *Learning and Instruction, 13,* 533–568.

Hattie, J. (2009). *Visible learning: A synthesis of over 800 meta-analyses relating to achievement.* New York, NY: Routledge.

Hunter, M. (1994). *Enhancing teaching.* New York, NY: Macmillan College Publishing.

Loveless, T. (2012). How well are American students learning? With sections on predicting the effect of the common core state standards, achievement gaps on the two NAEP tests, and misinterpreting international test scores. *The 2012 Brown Center Report on American Education, III*(1).

Metcalfe, J., & Shimamura, A. P. (1994). *Metacognition: Knowing about knowing.* Cambridge, MA: MIT Press.

National Governors Association Center for Best Practices & Council of Chief State School Officers. (2010). *Common core state standards.* Washington, DC: Authors.

Palincsar, A. S. (1986). Reciprocal teaching. In *Teaching reading as thinking.* Oak Brook, IL: North Central Regional Educational Laboratory.

Partnership for 21st Century Skills. (n.d.). *Framework for 21st century learning.* Retrieved from http://www.p21.org/overview

Peery, A. (2009). *Power strategies for effective teaching (seminar manual).* Englewood, CO: Lead + Learn Press.

Peery, A., Patrick, P., & Moore, D. (2013). *Ask, don't tell: Powerful questioning in the classroom.* Englewood, CO: Lead + Learn Press.

Popham, W. J. (2008). *Transformative assessment.* Alexandria, VA: ASCD.

PART TWO

Strategies in the Content Areas

CHAPTER SIX

Argumentative Writing:
The Core of Academic Success

Angela B. Peery

"... An ancient, accessible concept needs to be restored to its rightful place at the center of schooling: argument. In its various forms, it includes the ability to analyze and assess facts and evidence, support our solutions, and defend our interpretations and recommendations with clarity and precision—in every subject area. Argument is the primary skill essential to our success as citizens, students, and workers."

MIKE SCHMOKER and GERALD GRAFF, 2011

The Common Core State Standards have drawn teachers' attention to the one key skill that no university student, military officer, businessperson, or civil servant can do without: written argumentation. In the last decade or so, some educators had taken their eyes off this intellectual prize and had found themselves concentrating on multiple-choice questions (which often led to multiple-choice teaching) and short, constructed-response answers. Performance assessments and lengthy written compositions have been much more rare than in the pre-NCLB era (Darling-Hammond, 2010; Gallagher, 2009; Learning 24/7, 2005; Schmoker, 2006). The Common Core has refocused teachers on critical academic skills such as close reading, citing evidence, and writing logical argument like no other force could.

Many scholars and reformers welcome this refocusing, perhaps more than classroom practitioners do. However, most educators recognize that "generous amounts of reading, writing, and argument are essential to the development of truly literate and educated students" (Schmoker, 2006). So, while they may be confused or concerned about how to use more argumentation in their instruction, they realize the challenge is a worthy one.

The big idea here is simple. Logical argument is at the heart of academic discourse; thus, in order for students to be successful in college and in life, they must master the art of argumentation, and their teachers must be their guides.

ARGUMENT versus PERSUASION

As George Hillocks (2011) notes, "Argument is not simply a dispute, as when people disagree with one another or yell at each other. Argument is about making a case in support of a claim in everyday affairs" (p. xv). Teachers must first understand this nuanced definition and differentiate it from its more recognizable and prevalent cousin, persuasion. Then they must help their students understand argumentation in a multifaceted way and move them through a learning progression that starts with stating an opinion (in kindergarten), continues with making a logical claim (in sixth grade), and ends with writing sophisticated arguments that support claims, rebut counterclaims, and provide deep analysis (high school).

The Common Core documents themselves devote space to explaining what argumentation is, why it is important, and how it differs from stating one's opinions and attempting to persuade. Pages 23 through 25 of Appendix A of the English language arts and literacy standards discuss writing in general, the writing standards in particular, and the differences between persuasion and argumentation. One of the most important sentences in the entire expanse of text is the second one on page 23: "An argument is a reasoned, logical way of demonstrating that the writer's position, belief, or conclusion is valid" (National Governors Association Center for Best Practices and Council of Chief State School Officers, 2010). This sentence bears returning to over and over again, as it distills argumentative writing to its essence by focusing on its core ingredients, reason and logic. It also covers not only informational argumentation, which takes a problem or situation and provides at least one viable solution, but also literary analysis, in which the writer analyzes a work and stakes out a position on its worth or draws conclusions and supports them.

This same paragraph ends with a reminder that while young children (in grades kindergarten through 5) are not ready for presenting full-blown written arguments, they do possess the prerequisite skills. The document notes, "... They develop a variety of methods to extend and elaborate their work by providing examples, offering reasons for their assertions, and explaining cause and effect. These kinds of expository structures are steps on the road to argument" (NGACBP and CCSSO, 2010, p. 23). The steps toward formal argument are clearly laid out in the standards and supported in Appendix A.

On page 24 of Appendix A, a shaded box appears. This feature is worthy of careful study by individuals and collaborative groups. It succinctly highlights the differences between persuasion and argumentation—differences that are often difficult for even experienced teachers to delineate. Many English language arts and writing teachers have taught their students various rhetorical devices, such as the bandwagon approach, ad hominem attacks, and plain folks testimonials. Indeed, such devices have been a mainstay of upper elementary and middle school writing for more than 20 years, if my own teaching and hundreds of observations of other educators are a reliable indication. However, these types of devices should not consume valuable instructional time in the Common Core–aligned classroom. As noted in the shaded box, "A logical argument . . . convinces the audience because of the perceived merit and reasonableness of the claims and proofs offered rather than either the emotions the writing evokes in the audience or the character or credentials of the writer" (NGACBP and CCSSO, 2010, p. 24). Clearly, of the modes of persuasion that are as old as Aristotle, teachers must focus squarely on logos (logic, facts, data) and not pathos (appeals to emotion) or ethos (credibility of the writer). Pathos and ethos have been the focus of much persuasive writing and speaking, certainly in the middle grades, for years. Allowing students to showcase their ample skills in pathos and ethos has made for interesting projects, catchy videos, beautiful posters, and in some cases, effective writing, but it seems this focus has ill prepared them for the kinds of writing they must master for college and careers.

OPINION IN THE EARLY GRADES: THE FOUNDATION

In kindergarten, the Common Core argumentative writing standard appropriately begins as dictating, drawing, or writing. The students must "compose opinion pieces in which they tell a reader the topic or the name of the book they are writing about and state an opinion or preference about the topic or book." These activities are entirely appropriate for kindergartners and make clear to teachers exactly what is expected in terms of performance.

In grade 1, this writing standard becomes more rigorous, as students must supply a reason for the opinion that is held. Additionally, in their writing at this level, they must "provide a sense of closure." Again, the standard is developmentally appropriate, and the expectations are specific and clear. This standard at grade 1 seems to call for two or more related sentences of opinion and support.

In grade 2, the standard becomes even more complex, as students are required to "state an opinion, supply reasons that support the opinion, use linking words (e.g., *because*, *and*, *also*) to connect opinion and reasons, and provide a concluding statement or section." One reason is no longer sufficient; multiple reasons must exist for the opinion that is held. Notice also that the grade 2 standard clearly lays out what seems to be the skeleton for a sound opinion paragraph. Can a second grader write an opinion paragraph that contains two or more reasons to support the opinion? Of course! And this standard holds that up as the clear expectation.

In grades 3–5, the standard changes slightly. The term "point of view" is used herein in addition to the word "opinion." In this way, the standard is expanded and is moving ever closer to the grade

6 standard of stating a verifiable, arguable claim. Also, the word "information" is added at grade 4: "Write opinion pieces on topics or texts, supporting a point of view with reasons and information." Just stating reasons was enough previously, but in grades 4 and 5, one's personal reasons are not of the utmost importance. Writers must seek other information, outside the self, to support the opinions stated. This demand makes clear that students are now writing answers that are rooted in text and in the opinions and ideas of others—not just in the self.

The grade 5 standard in its entirety reads as follows:

> Write opinion pieces on topics or texts, supporting a point of view with reasons and information.
>
> a. Introduce a topic or text clearly, state an opinion, and create an organizational structure in which ideas are logically grouped to support the writer's purpose.
>
> b. Provide logically ordered reasons that are supported by facts and details.
>
> c. Link opinion and reasons using words, phrases, and clauses (e.g., *consequently, specifically*).
>
> d. Provide a concluding statement or section related to the opinion presented.

Students completing elementary school and achieving this standard are well prepared for the demands of future academic study. They have learned to write multiple paragraphs that focus on an opinion and to support that opinion with logically ordered information. They have learned to use transition words and phrases to link the parts of their composition, and they have learned to end in a way that makes it clear to the reader that they are done. Most middle school teachers would welcome these students with open arms and encouraging smiles and would be ready to take them further into argument.

THE MIDDLE YEARS: LAYING THE GROUNDWORK FOR COLLEGE SUCCESS

The argumentative writing standard becomes incredibly rigorous in grades 6–8. If eighth graders truly master the Common Core argumentative writing standard at their level, they will enter high school as competent writers and can further refine their skills in preparation for university-level work or entry-level employment.

The base standard in this span has become "Write arguments to support claims with clear reasons and relevant evidence." This statement contains five indicators underneath at each grade level. These indicators, as in earlier grades, lay out specifics about the content and the organization of each argumentative composition.

What is most interesting about this grade span is the fact that the rigor and complexity of the argument changes very specifically. In grade 6, a student writer makes a claim and supports it with reasons and evidence. (The word "evidence" is new at this grade level; the word at grade 5 is "information.") In grade 7, the writer must make a claim and then "acknowledge alternate or opposing claims." Being able to look at the issue or topic from alternate points of view is quite a rigorous expectation for pubescent students who live in the world of the self. And, in grade 8, the expectation ramps up further. At this level, the student must make a claim, support it, acknowledge other claims, and "distinguish the claim(s) from alternate or opposing claims." Now we are squarely in the world of effective rebuttal. As a former college instructor who had to teach argumentative writing to students who ranged in age from 18 to 55, I can attest to the fact that effectively providing rebuttals to counterclaims is difficult for any writer. But for an eighth grade writer, that is going to be a feat! However, with some of the fifth grade and middle school argumentative writing I have already seen as teachers are grappling with the Common Core, I'm absolutely positive this feat can be accomplished.

HIGH SCHOOL: REFINING ARGUMENTATIVE SKILLS

When students who have had Common Core–aligned instruction in middle school enter high school, they should be well prepared to attack argumentative writing at a deeper level. The main standard for grade bands 9–10 and 11–12 is, "Write arguments to support claims in an analysis of substantive topics or texts, using valid reasoning and relevant and sufficient evidence." The word "substantive" is new, and the explicit connection to texts, which implies argumentative literary analysis, is also new. Otherwise, there is very little in this standard or its indicators that was not done in middle school.

The idea of fairness appears in grade band 9–10: "Develop claim(s) and counterclaims fairly, supplying evidence for each while pointing out the strengths and limitations of both in a manner that anticipates the audience's knowledge level and concerns." In grade band 11–12, thoroughness is also an expectation: "Develop claim(s) and counterclaims fairly and thoroughly, supplying the most relevant evidence for each while pointing out the strengths and limitations of both in a manner that anticipates the audience's knowledge level, concerns, values, and possible biases." Cohesion, formal style, objective tone, and attention to the conventions of the discipline being written within are also important. However, most writing teachers would likely agree with me that these issues are minor in comparison to the "biggies" that were laid out in grades 6–8; that is, stating a claim and acknowledging and rebutting opposing claims are far more difficult than refining one's writing stylistically.

Argumentative writing is certainly very important in the high school grades, and it should be done frequently not only in the English language arts classroom, but also in science, history and social studies, and the technical subjects, as the Common Core standards call for. However, the overarching goal in high school seems to be to provide students with ample practice in writing arguments, thereby helping them refine their arguments, so that they are indeed "college-ready." So, while high school is the place for argumentation to reach its fullest application in the K–12 system, the foundation for college-level argumentative writing is laid in grades 6–8. Grades 9–12 are for the application of argument widely and broadly, and for the refinement of the writing itself.

INSTRUCTIONAL IMPLICATIONS

Mike Schmoker (2011) has made recommendations for writing in general, and these recommendations easily mesh with the expectations of the writing strand of the Common Core and with the expectations for written argumentation.

He starts by advocating several formal papers starting in second grade—about one per month or about nine per year, written in at least two drafts. This is developmentally appropriate and also honors the writing process. For elementary teachers and students, who have English language arts time every single day, this amount of writing is doable. I would add to his expectations that of these approximately nine compositions, no more than three should be narrative structure. There has been an imbalance of narrative writing to informative and argumentative (opinion) in elementary schools for years (Reeves, 2005), and this imbalance must be addressed, particularly in grades 2 and 3, as students move toward higher and higher nonfiction (and "nonstory") writing expectations.

Schmoker's expectations for the upper elementary grades and middle and high school years don't change—still about nine papers per year, written in two or more drafts. This expectation is actually low if we consider the time students spend in English language arts classes. In those classes alone, one major composition per marking period should be an absolute minimum, and that expectation alone would yield four to six papers. If we add to that several major papers in social studies, science, and other subjects each year, students should be in double digits. This is not unreasonable; however, it has been rare for students to write in high volume in high school. As just one compelling example, in 2003, 75 percent of students reported they did not write *at all* in their history or social studies courses (ASCD SmartBrief). As author and teacher Kelly Gallagher (2006) notes, "There is a literacy stampede bearing down on our students, yet the skill of writing . . . is being badly shortchanged in our schools. To make matters worse, this neglect of writing is coming at a time when the writing demands required in the real world are intensifying. Students are writing less when they desperately need to be writing more. A lot more" (p. 169).

Schmoker has also offered a simple argumentative writing template that would be easy to use with students in grades 6–12. It is summarized below:

- Read a text or texts very carefully.
- Based on your reading, make a claim.
- Summarize the objections to your claim.
- Make one point at a time.
- Support your claim.
- Address the objections.
- Write clearly enough so that *virtually anyone* can understand what you have written.

The first two bullets align nicely with the Common Core's urging to have students engage in close reading and read multiple texts on a given topic or issue. The third, fifth, and sixth bullets represent the expectations in grades 6–8 very clearly: claim, opposing claims, rebuttal. And the fourth and seventh bullets are simply good advice about writing. I believe any teacher of grade 4 or above could use this template with their students to guide the writing of effective arguments.

GET STARTED TOMORROW

So, what can teachers start doing tomorrow to address argumentative writing? First, know the standard for your grade level. Understand the differences between opinion, persuasion, and argumentation, and know when these differences are critical.

Second, establish a learning environment that encourages argumentation *daily*. This means frequently asking students, "What is your point of view on that?" or "Can you take a position on that?"

Then ask for the support. This is vastly different from many of the most common questions I hear in classrooms, such as, "How do you feel about that?" and "What do you wonder about?" These might be fine questions, especially for discussions of literature, but they need to be coupled with more prodding from an argumentative or critical literacy stance. We must start asking our students to take stands and make claims and support those statements with ample evidence—not with feeling, conjecture, and wonder.

Third, students must write—a *lot.* Short opinion pieces should be completed at least weekly in grades 2–5, coupled with longer pieces that go through the writing process, at least once every couple of months. (Other types of writing are occurring in the alternating months.) In middle and high school, students should be engaged in argumentative discussion almost daily in most subjects, but certainly in English language arts. In English class, they should be writing short informal argumentative pieces every few days, and longer more complex pieces every marking period. The possibilities for interdisciplinary work abound and should be considered.

As Mike Schmoker (2006) has said, "... Substantive reading, writing, and talking are exceedingly rare in most classrooms. We need to be alarmed by this fact" (p. 54). Argumentative writing, and the speaking, listening, and reading that occur alongside it, are the cornerstone of academic literacy. Our students need more experience with argumentative writing than they have ever had before in order to be prepared for college and careers. Armed with the rigorous demands of the Common Core State Standards, and the impetus among both teachers and other educational leaders to help students succeed, we can give it to them.

References

ASCD SmartBrief. (2003, March 16). Term papers no longer a major focus. Retrieved from http://www.smartbrief.com/servlet/ArchiveServlet?issueid=5F3831E2-3109-4B2E-A6EB-8DD19A8538EE&lmid=archives

Darling-Hammond, L. (2010). *The flat world and education: How America's commitment to equity will determine our future.* New York, NY: Teachers College Press.

Gallagher, K. (2006). *Teaching adolescent writers.* Portland, ME: Stenhouse.

Gallagher, K. (2009). *Readicide: How schools are killing reading and what you can do about it.* Portland, ME: Stenhouse.

Hillocks, G. (2011). *Teaching argument writing, grades 6–12: Supporting claims with relevant evidence and clear reasoning.* Portsmouth, NH: Heinemann.

Learning 24/7. (2005, April 7). *Classroom observation study.* Study presented at the meeting of the National Conference on Standards and Assessment in Las Vegas, NV.

National Governors Association Center for Best Practices & Council of Chief State School Officers (NGACBP & CCSSO). (2010). *Common core state standards.* Washington, DC: Authors.

Reeves, D. B. (2005). *101 questions & answers about standards, assessment, and accountability.* Englewood, CO: Lead + Learn Press.

Schmoker, M. (2006). *Results now: How we can achieve unprecedented improvements in teaching and learning.* Alexandria, VA: ASCD.

Schmoker, M. (2011). *Focus: Elevating the essentials to radically improve student learning.* Alexandria, VA: ASCD.

Schmoker, M., & Graff, G. (2011, April). More argument, fewer standards. *Education Week, 30*(28), 31, 33.

CHAPTER SEVEN

Meaningful Reading for Critical Thinking

Lisa Cebelak

"…We don't learn to read well by being taught reading skills. We learn to read well by reading a lot for meaning: to analyze or support arguments, to arrive at our own opinions as we make inferences or attempt to solve problems."

MICHAEL SCHMOKER, 2011

MULTIPLE TEXTS FOR DEEPER UNDERSTANDING

Think about the last time you needed to know something and no one was around to give you the answer. What did you do? Most of us turn to the Internet for answers as a starting point. What is the best brand and best price for an item? What is the political issue of the day and why are people so divided about it? What can I do to turn off the "maintenance check" alert light in my car without having to take it in to a dealership? And what will happen if I turn it off myself and skip the service call? Most of us would not rely on only one source for the answer. For instance, when comparing brands and prices, one would want to look up different reviews and ratings from multiple sources, and certainly not rely only on a single brand's Web site. When trying to gain perspective about a political issue, one would most likely view multiple sites to understand different perspectives and not rely on just one news source. And, when reading up on the pesky "check engine" light that comes on every 25,000 miles, one would first have to look up the make and model of the car and many mechanic pages that specifically deal with the problem at hand. Think about it. How much reading and what type of reading do you do that relies on multiple sources for you to make informed decisions?

READING AND THE COMMON CORE

The Common Core State Standards were released in 2010 and have been adopted by a large majority of U.S. states and territories. Much has been written about the English language arts and literacy Common Core standards—especially about the reading standards. The reading strand is separated into three categories: reading foundational skills (K–5 only), reading literature, and reading informational texts. At the secondary level (6–12), the reading strand separates by discipline outside of ELA into reading for literacy in history/social studies, and reading for literacy in science and technical subjects. The emphasis in the reading strand has been "text complexity" and "close reading." Other "newer" nods to Common Core reading have been reading for evidence, literary nonfiction, and academic vocabulary. Going beyond these categories, one must pause and think: "How do I read in today's society?" "What are the

standards that support this question?" and "How does this change
or reinforce instructional practices in the classroom?"

In close reading, students reread the same text over and over
again. The student does not just read through the text once and
move on, but re-examines the text at a deeper level. Close reading
is a strategy or skill needed for students to navigate difficult texts.
But we must not stop there. The next step is to build on that skill
of critical thinking by applying it to more than one text at a time.
In the real world, we often read multiple sources about a topic and
have to analyze that material to make informed decisions. Isn't this
what we do as consumers? Is this not a part of our daily life? What
has changed over the years is the fact that the Internet allows us to
do this at a much more rapid pace. In society today, we reference
everything. We want to stay informed. The Internet keeps us connected to the content, but it is up to us to navigate the information,
accept or reject it, and learn what is valid or not along the way. The
Internet has created a need for the ability to sort and sift through
information at a more rapid pace than in the past. In the academic
setting, we have great works of literature, nonfiction articles, U.S.
government documents, and other print sources that are part of
this process, but we also must acknowledge that "multi-media"
sources are expanding by the minute. How digital content changes
the role of reading in the classroom must be addressed.

The key design considerations section of the ELA Common
Core states (National Governors Association Center for Best Practices and Council of Chief State School Officers, 2010, p. 4):

> To be ready for college, workforce training, and life in a tech-
> nological society, students need the ability to gather, com-
> prehend, evaluate, synthesize and report on information and

ideas, to conduct original research in order to answer questions or solve problems, and to analyze and create a high volume and extensive range of print and nonprint texts in media forms old and new. The need to conduct research and to produce and consume media is embedded into every aspect of today's curriculum. In like fashion, research and media skills and understandings are embedded throughout the Standards rather than treated in a separate section.

Students today need to be able to do more than gather and comprehend information. They must also be able to wield higher-order thinking skills, such as evaluating and synthesizing a plethora of information to inform their decisions.

Integration of Knowledge and Ideas for Literature

In the Common Core State Standards, reading multiple texts first comes into play in the standards for second grade. Common Core RL.2.9 states: "Compare and contrast two or more versions of the same story by different authors or from different cultures." Students will first have to understand and comprehend each story, and then analyze the two stories and their relationship to each other. Close reading might be needed for each individual story, but that is a repeated strategy or skill learned at an early age. In second grade, students are realizing that different texts on the same topic can be compared and contrasted. The skills mentioned in this standard will be built upon to later include "texts in different forms or genres in terms of their approaches to similar themes and topics" in sixth grade, and will increase in complexity such that in eleventh and twelfth grade, students must "demonstrate knowledge of eighteenth-, nineteenth-, and early-twentieth-century foundational works of American literature, including how two or more texts from the same period treat similar themes or topics." In literature, students need to know that it is important to read more than one text on a topic or theme. They need to learn the critical thinking skills that start with comparing and contrasting, but they must also be analytical readers and thinkers. When students focus on multiple texts, they gain a broader perspective, are able to dig deeper into the content or topic at hand, and early on gain the understanding that not only are there multiple sources to read, but that reading multiple sources on one topic and learning to synthesize them allows for richer meaning and thinking.

Integration of Knowledge and Ideas for Informational Text

In the informational text reading strand, students start looking at multiple texts on a topic in kindergarten. Common Core standard RI.K.9 states: "With prompting and support, identify basic similarities in and differences between two texts on the same topic." The skill in the standard—what students should be able to do—changes to "compare and contrast" by second grade, echoing the literature standard, but in this standard, in second grade students are "comparing and contrasting the most important points." I would argue that this is higher-order thinking. One must first closely read one text and analyze it to evaluate what is most important, and then do the same with the other text. Once this has occurred, the student must then synthesize the information of the two texts and re-evaluate what is most important. By fourth grade, the term "integrate" replaces "compare and contrast" and students are required to write or speak about the subject, and in fifth grade the "two texts" wording is replaced with "several texts." For clarity, RI.5.9 reads "integrate information from several texts on the same topic in order to write or speak about the subject knowledgeably." Also, in fifth grade, RI.5.7 calls for multiple sources by stating that students should be able to "draw on multiple print or digital sources, demonstrating the ability to locate an answer to a question quickly or to solve a problem efficiently." These standards go hand-in-hand and represent real-world application. This is college- and career-readiness at its best. This is applicable for literature, informational text, and all types of multimedia.

At the secondary level, the standard continues in complexity by requiring students in eighth grade (RI.8.9) to "analyze a case in which two or more texts provide conflicting information on the same topic and identify where the texts disagree on matters of fact or interpretation." Although the skill being stated is "analyze," it is apparent that students must first closely read each text and then be able to identify where there is conflicting information. By eleventh and twelfth grade, students must be able to "integrate and evaluate multiple sources of information presented in different media or formats as well as in words in order to address a question or solve a problem" (RI.11–12.9).

The emphasis on multiple sources and being able to critically think at higher levels is a repeated theme in the Common Core. In the literacy standards for history/social studies, science, and technical subjects, reading multiple texts on a topic is perhaps seen as even more complex than in the language arts standards. In the history/social studies literacy standards, by grades 11–12, students will need to be able to integrate and evaluate multiple sources of information in both print and digital text. And, not only do they need to be able to integrate information from diverse sources, but they also need to note discrepancies among sources, including primary and secondary sources. While this requirement is similar in the science and technical subjects literacy standards, those standards state that after students synthesize the information from a range of sources, they should be able to resolve conflicting information when possible. How can we prepare our students to resolve a problem or issue when in many cases there is no clear-cut answer or solution? This type of critical thinking in reading is college- and career-readiness personified. It is innovation. This is what it means to be literate in the 21st century.

SMARTER ASSESSMENTS

In the past, it hasn't been easy to test this type of reading. It is time-consuming for students to read multiple texts, and it takes a human scorer to be able to analyze student answers, because they tend to be extended constructed-response questions. Next generation assessment groups have gone on the record as stating that they will assess this type of reading of multiple texts through performance-based tasks. Both the Smarter Balanced Assessment Consortium (SBAC) and the Partnership for Assessment of Readiness for College and Careers (PARCC) have even released test item samples of performance tasks at multiple grade levels. The Smarter Balanced Assessment Consortium (2012) defines a performance task as:

> Performance tasks challenge students to apply their knowledge and skills to respond to complex real-world problems. They can best be described as collections of questions and activities that are coherently connected to a single theme or scenario. These activities are meant to measure capacities

such as depth of understanding, research skills, and complex analysis, which cannot be adequately assessed with traditional assessment questions.

The test item samples provided by SBAC for three grade levels (4, 6, and 11) all contain performance tasks that instruct students to examine several sources. Some of the sources are print, and some are multimedia. Students will need to synthesize information from multiple sources and write to answer a question that is posed. PARCC also has performance-based components. One is a literary analysis task, while another is a research simulation task. PARCC states that the latter component "asks students to exercise the career and college readiness skills of observation, deduction, and proper use and evaluation of evidence across text types" (2013). The examples of the research task ask students to analyze an informational topic presented in multiple formats. PARCC included video clips and other multimedia in their examples beyond print articles. What is key to both assessments is that both groups call for students to examine several sources. Students need to be able to read and compare multiple texts or other forms of media on the same topic and know how to be critical thinkers. This isn't just a skill needed for a state assessment; this is a lifelong skill that is needed to be a discerning reader in today's world.

STRATEGIES FOR READING MULTIPLE TEXTS

Most educators find themselves having to shift their classroom instruction to meet the rigor of the Common Core State Standards. When focusing in on the reading standards, teachers will need to rethink how they can deliver a topic using multiple texts. This tends to be easiest with informational text. A teacher could have a topic that is controversial and could find different books and articles (print and/or digital) for students, and even include video clips, political cartoons, or advertisements. A textbook cannot be the only source in the classroom anymore. More than ever, a textbook is really just "another source" in the classroom. And what about novels or plays? As stated earlier, reading multiple texts on a topic is also included in the literature reading standards. What does this look like in the classroom? PARCC shares this information as food for thought: "Students will analyze an informational topic presented through several articles or multimedia stimuli, the first text being an anchor text that introduces the topic" (2013). A classic such as Shakespeare's *Romeo and Juliet* could be introduced to the class as an anchor text. The topic or theme from this classic could focus on marriage when parents disapprove. The educator might share an article on the history of arranged marriages, a scientific article on teenagers and parental involvement, and a factual document on state marriage age laws. Think about all the different resources you could find on this topic and how this might actually increase student engagement in the classroom. Instead of reading *Romeo and Juliet* and "moving on" once the play is over, consider reading that classic along with many other texts that present different viewpoints on a single theme or topic. Performance tasks are meant to be real-world scenarios that get the students' attention because someone is finally addressing the "why" instead of just the "what." If we want to have discerning readers, we need to give them something to get excited about. If we want students to read multiple texts on a topic or issue, we need to give them a topic or issue that is relevant. If we want students to be college- and career-ready, we must start including more multiple-text activities, including activities involving multimedia texts, in our classrooms and allowing time for students to closely read and grapple with not just one text, but with many texts on a single topic. After all, isn't this how we read in the real world?

References

National Governors Association Center for Best Practices & Council of Chief State School Officers. (2010). *Common core state standards for English language arts & literacy in history/social studies, science, and technical subjects.* Washington, DC: Authors.

Partnership for Assessment of Readiness for College and Careers. (2013). Grade 3 summative assessment, performance-based component, research simulation task. Retrieved from http://www.parcconline.org/samples/english-language-artsliteracy/grade-3-elaliteracy

Schmoker, M. (2011). *Focus: Elevating the essentials to radically improve student learning.* Alexandria, VA: ASCD.

Smarter Balanced Assessment Consortium. (2012). *Smarter balanced assessments.* Retrieved from http://www.smarterbalanced.org/smarter-balanced-assessments/

CHAPTER EIGHT

The Engaging Math Class:

A Place Everyone Wants To Be

Lori Cook

"In addition to selecting tasks with goals in mind and sharing essential information, the teacher's primary role is to establish a classroom culture that supports learning with understanding, thereby serving to motivate students to learn."

NATIONAL RESEARCH COUNCIL, 2001, p. 345

For many decades, math classes have been a place where teachers do all of the work. They plan the lessons, teach the lessons, model the problems, and sometimes even answer their own questions. Teachers leave exhausted at the end of the day and students leave wondering why they were there. Students are actually turned off by mathematics due to this lack of engagement. I like to call it the Charlie Brown syndrome: "Wha, wha, wha, wha"—too much teacher talk, and all the students hear is "wha, wha, wha...." Fortunately, the Common Core authors created the mathematical practice standards using two major pieces of research, the *Principles and Standards for School Mathematics* (2000) by the National Council of Teachers of Mathematics and *Adding It Up!* (2001) by the National Research Council. The Standards for Mathematical Practice are not *what* students should learn, but *how* students should learn and how students should interact with the content. The eight mathematical practices are as follows (National Governors Association Center for Best Practices and Council of Chief State School Officers, 2010, pp. 7–8):

1. Make sense of problems and persevere in solving them.

2. Reason abstractly and quantitatively.

3. Construct viable arguments and critique the reasoning of others.

4. Model with mathematics.

5. Use appropriate tools strategically.

6. Attend to precision.

7. Look for and make use of structure.

8. Look for and express regularity in repeated reasoning.

These practices are revolutionizing math classrooms across the country. No longer are math classes teacher-centered and teacher-driven; instead, they are becoming places that require students to reason, to interact with content and each other, and to justify solutions, as well as a place that fosters deep understanding of the mathematics, not merely a regurgitation of procedural steps. These are very exciting times to be a math teacher and math student.

Yet, with this excitement comes apprehension and insecurity for many teachers. A frequent question I hear is, "If I don't tell them how to solve a problem, how will they learn?" Teachers struggle with letting go, and students struggle with thinking at higher levels, because they have been told what to do and how to think for so many years. Students who are not comfortable taking their prior knowledge and using it to discover mathematics become frustrated with the teacher and push back, and some even say, "It's your job to teach me, so tell me what to do next." I have observed this happen in both elementary and secondary classes. I actually had a student stop in the middle of a problem-solving experience, push back the problem, and say, "I quit, Ms. Cook, give me a worksheet. I am tired of thinking." This student had never been required to think and reason in a math class at this level for an extended period of time. She was very frustrated that I wouldn't tell her the next step. Instead, I asked leading questions to allow her to discover the mathematics. Developing perseverance and the ability to solve problems quickly became a priority and focus in my classroom. This didn't happen overnight, but once students understood the expectations, realized that this approach to learning mathematics is engaging, and "tasted" success, they began pushing themselves. Before I knew it, students were racing to math class instead of running away.

I associate problem solving with working out when explaining it to my students. I couldn't bench press 150 pounds the first time I went to the gym. After many weeks of lifting dumbbells, I was able to begin bench pressing just the bar. Eventually I added weights and finally was able to bench press 150 pounds. Problem solving is like lifting weights: students must build their confidence and develop perseverance by solving problems frequently and by increasing the rigor of those problems gradually. Not unlike developing the ability to bench press, this requires scaffolding of tasks as well as providing structures that allow for engagement with the content and with other students.

The National Research Council discovered in their research that the teaching and learning of mathematics is the "product of interactions among the teacher, the students, and the mathematics" (2001, p. 313). In too many American classes, the students have been bystanders. But the Common Core mathematical practice standards force students to engage with the mathematics, with other students, and with the teacher. The "opportunity to learn," described as "circumstances that allow students to engage in and spend time on academic tasks such as working on problems, exploring situations and gathering data, listening to explanations, reading texts, or conjecturing and justifying" (National Research Council, 2001, pp. 333–334), needs to be the focus of every teacher.

To create a classroom that requires interaction between teachers, students, and content on a continual cycle, teachers will need to assess their roles in the classroom. It is the job of the teacher to choose content, decide the appropriate format, and determine how the students will engage with the content. Will they explore new situations through problem solving, gather data, read texts, listen to explanations, ask probing questions, and/or make conjectures? (National Research Council, 2001, pp. 333–334). Teachers must become the activators (Hattie, 2009, p. 243) of student learning and create opportunities for students to engage with the mathematics in meaningful ways. To build capacity, teachers must create success by providing structures that guide students and provide opportunities to use the mathematical practices. For this to occur, the learning environment must be one that promotes respect for differing ideas and one that welcomes mistakes. Building a classroom that acts as a community of learners involves four important ideas (National Research Council, 2001, pp. 344–345):

1. All ideas and approaches are valued. Students must respect all ideas and responses shared by classmates and realize they are possible contributions to everyone's learning.

2. Students have the freedom to explore alternative strategies, choose a method that makes sense to them, and share the method(s) of solving problems and their thinking and reasoning with the rest of the class.

3. Mistakes are valued and are seen as opportunities for everyone to examine reasoning and to learn from error analysis.

4. Justification of solutions is required and the resolution of disagreements exists in mathematical arguments. The logic and structure of the subject is required and is not based on the popularity of the person presenting the solution.

DAILY PROBLEM SOLVING

For a community of learners to thrive, mathematical discourse must become a daily occurrence in the math classroom. Unfortunately, many math classrooms have been sterile and one-sided for many years. Teachers who have tried creating collaborative conversations (math discourse) tell me frequently that the students won't talk about math. They have tried, and the students are silent or talk about their weekend plans. For many students, this happens because they don't know how to talk about math and they've never been given a reason for talking about math. The older they are and the longer they have been forced to sit quietly and take notes, the less equipped they are to ask questions of the mathematics. "Learning is stimulated by a need to solve an interesting problem, and it culminates with new insights about mathematics" (Ben-Hur, 2006, p. 77). It is the job of the math teacher to teach students how to talk about math and to provide opportunities that will peak their curiosity. Instead of telling and showing students a procedure or formula, providing guided practice problems, and culminating with a few word problems on the bottom of the homework sheet (which, by the way, my students always skipped), we should create meaning for the mathematics by creating a problem that will "hook" the students. Before direct instruction, pose a problem that there are multiple ways to solve, and possibly multiple answers for, depending upon the justification provided by the students. Provide students with manipulatives, graph paper, calculators, and any other resource or tool that might be needed. Let go and allow the students to struggle, discuss possible approaches with each other, discover the answer, and have fun.

By starting each new lesson with a question that students can struggle with, student engagement increases and students make specific connections to direct instruction that they will receive the following day. Ben-Hur (2006, pp. 75–76) lists the following advantages for students who are engaged in problem-based learning:

- Promotion of active involvement
- Facilitation of intrinsic motivation, excitement, and challenge instead of boredom
- Development of meaning

- Engagement in purposeful learning
- Promotion of greater concentration and persistence; increased time on task
- Direct practice with mathematical concepts before symbols and recording
- Engagement of thinking
- Facilitation of repetition without tedium
- Encouragement of self-regulation and monitoring
- Perception among all students that they have an equal likelihood of success
- Inherent enjoyment and success that foster positive attitudes about the self and about mathematics
- Stimulation of creativity and imagination and encouragement of cooperative learning
- Stimulation of classroom dialogue, communication, and the development of interpersonal skills

Many teachers ask where they can find problems that match their unit focus and will require problem solving. There are a plethora of word problems available in textbooks, but most of them provide too much information and become computation within text. A lot of problems provide step-by-step guidance and lead students to the answer. But we can, as Dan Meyer (2010) suggests, remove all of the excess helps that are included in traditional word problems, find the essence of the question, and allow students to solve problems. Compare and contrast these two problems:

Nicholas' Cage

Mr. Robinson is building a new cage for his rabbit, Nicholas. He has 12 feet of fencing to build the rabbit cage. The cage needs to be a rectangle. What are the lengths and widths of the different sizes of cages that he can make with that amount of fencing? Which cage will give Nicholas the largest area to play around in?

Nicholas' Cage Revised

Mr. Robinson is building a new cage for his rabbit, Nicholas. He has 12 feet of fencing. What are the dimensions of the cage that will give Nicholas the largest space to play in? Justify your final solution.

The first problem is a traditional word problem that is similar to those found in textbooks. By asking what the essence of the problem is and removing the specific steps to solve the problem, and/or the hints given, a preferred problem-solving situation occurs, as in the second example. Students are forced to become critical thinkers instead of regurgitating a procedure. By removing the idea that the cage must be a rectangle, students are allowed the opportunity to explore all shapes. By using the word "space" instead of "area," students are required to think about exactly what they need to find: area or perimeter. By using the word "dimensions" instead of "length and width," students encounter more math vocabulary and are not influenced by what the final shape should be. It doesn't matter what level of mathematics you teach; problems are waiting to be discovered. In a problem-solving situation, we want students to explore all possible options, decide which option best answers the question(s), and justify why they made that decision. Study the problems in your textbook and ask yourself:

- What is the question asking?
- What is the limited amount of information students need to explore the situation?
- What will force students to look at the problem from all different angles, make a final decision, and justify their reasoning?
- Is the question a step-by-step guide to finding an answer? If so, keep editing.

Taking problems and modifying them in this way will give students the opportunity to use the mathematical practices daily. Depending on the problems chosen and how you modify the problems, you could argue that students will need to use all practices. Looking at the revised "Nicolas' Cage" problem, the following mathematical practices will be required by students (NGACBP and CCSSO, 2010. pp. 7–8):

1. Make sense of problems and persevere in solving them.
    - There is more than one way to make the cage and students will need to persevere to find all of the options.
2. Reason abstractly and quantitatively.
    - Students will need to reason about the problem and decide which shape has the most space and prove it by representing them.

3. Construct viable arguments and critique the reasoning of others.

   • Justification of the solution is required and students within groups will need to agree on a solution.

4. Model with mathematics.

   • Students will either represent the cages with manipulatives or draw them on graph paper.

5. Use appropriate tools strategically.

   • Students will choose what tools to use to solve the problem.

6. Attend to precision.

   • To find the cage with the largest area, students will need to use precision in their calculations, and in their justifications they will need to use correct mathematical vocabulary.

7. Look for and make use of structure.

   • Students will begin discovering the attributes of area and will continue doing so in the direct instruction and application of the work.

8. Look for and express regularity in repeated reasoning.

   • Students may even begin to discover the area formulas through repeated exposure to finding all of the different areas of rectangles as well as triangles.

MATHEMATICAL DISCOURSE

In addition to being provided with the opportunity to discover meaning for the mathematics through the use of problem solving, many students need extra support talking about mathematics. Many students do not have the confidence it takes to talk about math, so they are reluctant to share their thinking with the class. Allowing students to answer questions with a partner or group before the whole-group discussion builds their confidence and increases their participation. The teacher's role is to guide the conversations by posing questions for the student groups to discuss. By asking the questions that follow, you will provide students with the opportunity to practice mathematical discourse, develop their skills, and gain confidence in their mathematical abilities.

1. What information is given and what is the problem asking?
   - Students find, highlight, and discuss the given information and the problem they will solve.

2. What strategy will you begin with, and why?
   - Students discuss their strategies and justify their choices.

3. What is the very first step you will do to solve the problem? Why? What is the next step you will do? Why? (Continue asking these questions until the problem is solved.)
   - Students stop and discuss each step they are doing and justify why they are doing it. It is important to note that sometimes students try a step and it doesn't work, so they need to choose another method. Mathematics involves trying

different methods and being willing to admit when a method doesn't work and moving on to try a different method. Learning from our mistakes is very powerful.

4. How did you get your solution and how do you know it is mathematically correct?
   - Students explain, step by step, the process they used to discover the final answer, and then they justify their answer. Encouraging students to determine whether their solution is a reasonable answer is very powerful at this stage.

Problem solving can be very challenging for students in the beginning. These questions help students learn the power of mathematical discourse as well as the power of metacognition (thinking about one's own thinking). It is very important for students to realize that all great problem solvers think about their thinking and struggle to find solutions. By using mathematical discourse, students become comfortable with the process and actually enjoy the opportunity to stretch themselves and become lifelong problem solvers.

THE POSTER METHOD

One problem-solving structure that became a favorite in my classrooms and in classrooms across the country is called "the poster method." This is a structure from *Five Easy Steps to a Balanced Math Program* by Larry Ainsworth and Jan Christinson (2011). This structure builds students' confidence and engagement by structuring problem solving with built-in layers of support. The key to the success of this structure is that the teacher's role is *not* to jump in and "save" students, but rather to activate their learning through questioning, and thus facilitate the learning experience in the classroom. This will need to be discussed with the students prior to the first poster method experience, and every time after that, until the students believe in themselves. The goal of the poster method is not only to build students' confidence, but also to change their mindset. It is important that students come to realize that problem solving takes time and is hard work, but is so much more rewarding than following a set of procedures given by the teacher. It is about the process of learning and the journey, not about the answer.

Poster Method Sequence

This sequence was developed by Larry Ainsworth and Jan Christinson (2011, p. 56).

1. **Individual work:** The teacher poses the problem and allows students to work silently and individually for about 3–5 minutes on their data sheets. (The data sheet is a blank piece of paper that students record all of their work on.) It is very important to tell the students you will be stopping them and that you do not expect an answer at that time.

2. **Summarize:** Students stop and summarize their work to this point in complete sentences. Students stand when they have summarized their work.

3. **Share:** Once everyone in the class is standing, the teacher chooses 2–3 students to read their summaries. Be careful not to allow the answer to get in

the room at this point. (This step allows those students who are struggling and who only read the problem several times to hear multiple approaches and build their confidence to attempt one of the possible approaches.)

4. **Group work:** The teacher thoughtfully groups students into small groups of three or four. Students sit and share their methods and work with their group. Students continue working on the problem together and discuss each step along the way. All students are still writing on their data sheets. Each group agrees on a solution.

5. **Group data sheet:** The teacher provides each group with a piece of chart paper, or a "poster," and students create a group data sheet. Each student's work must be on the poster and in each student's handwriting, whether correct or incorrect, to show a record of thought. (Some teachers have the students divide the poster and each student is assigned a portion to copy their data sheet onto. Others allow the students to decide where and how they are going to include all work and all handwriting.)

6. **Visit:** One student is selected to stay with the group poster and explain the work to the visitors. The other group members go out and "visit" other groups, investigating the reasoning and work of other groups. (In my class, the visitors were only allowed to ask questions of the person explaining the poster. This helps keep a respectful climate in the room.)

7. **Final answer:** Students return to their original group and share what they discovered. The group continues working, deciding whether they will use any information they gathered during their visits with other groups, and finalizes their answer.

8. **Written explanation:** When the group has a final answer, they turn their poster over and write an explanation in complete sentences that answers the following questions:
   • How did your group solve the problem?
   • How does your group know your solution is mathematically correct?

During this time, students are checking to make sure everyone in the group understands the work and solution and taking turns explaining the group's poster to prepare for the circle discussion. They do not know who will be chosen to present their group's poster.

9. **Circle discussion and final answer:** Students create a circle and stand with their group and poster. Each group shares only their solution in "whip around" fashion. Then the teacher chooses one member from each group to share their poster and the work required to find the solution. Students are encouraged to ask questions of each group. The teacher may need to model asking questions to create group discussions and share the reasoning behind the work of each group. When all groups have shared their posters, the posters are hung in the room or hallway

with all student names on each poster. The teacher concludes the poster method by sharing the correct answer or answers by using a poster from one of the groups.

The poster method is a structure that develops student voice, student belief in themselves and their ability, and student engagement. As with all great lessons, planning must occur before the structure is introduced. A few questions to ask to facilitate planning are:

- Does the problem relate to the current unit focus?
- Is the problem accessible to all students?
- Does the problem challenge mathematical understanding?
- Does the problem involve ideas from more than one mathematical strand?
- Do I understand the math in the problem?
- Have I planned questions to use when students are "stuck"?

The teacher's role is to emphasize mathematical reasoning, stress verification and use of math vocabulary, believe that students have the capacity to solve problems, ask questions to activate the students' learning instead of "saving" the students, train students in the components of the process, build student capacity to solve problems by implementing problem solving regularly, and become a problem solver yourself (Ainsworth and Christinson, 2011, p. 55). Many teachers complain that they do not have time to teach problem solving in their classrooms, but once they try the poster method, they see the benefits and many incorporate it into their weekly plans to reinforce learning. Problem solving is an integral part of the mathematics classroom, and when it is implemented thoughtfully, the students will be asking for more.

SELF-EVALUATION AND TEACHER COLLABORATION

As teachers, we need to step back and evaluate our practices and the learning environment in which we are expecting students to "learn math." For some, this is very uncomfortable, but it is a necessary undertaking. Our students are probably not the same type of students that we were, and more than likely they have different needs than we did. Hattie discusses the power of "microteaching" and the effect it has on teaching and learning in his revolutionary work *Visible Learning: A Synthesis of Over 800 Meta-Analyses Relating to Achievement* (2009). Microteaching, with a high effect size of 0.88 (calculating to over two years of student growth), traditionally involves student teachers in a laboratory setting, instructing a small group of students, and afterwards preservice teachers with an advisor debriefing the effectiveness of the lesson. Many times the lessons are videotaped for further study and discussions, allowing for individuals to evaluate the effectiveness of the teaching practices and learning that occurred (Hattie, 2009, p. 112). Lesson study, which allows for continuous improvement and learning, is where classroom teachers (veteran and novice) come together to focus on several "research lessons" over a period of time (anywhere from several months to a year). Stigler and Hiebert, in *The Teaching Gap* (1999, pp.121–126), identify several key features and benefits of lesson study:

1. Based on a long-term continuous improvement model

2. Maintains a constant focus on student learning

3. Focuses on the direct improvement of teaching in context

4. Is collaborative

5. Allows teachers to see themselves as contributing to the development of knowledge about teaching as well as to their own professional development

The use of lesson study and microteaching will enhance the implementation of the mathematical practices and evaluate the "opportunity to learn" that is present in the classroom. Implementation of the lesson study format by teachers facilitates the discussion of the following issues that are directly connected to how students learn mathematics:

1. The ratio between teacher voice and student voice

2. How students are engaging with the content and each other

3. How often students are making conjectures and justifying their thinking

4. The type and level of questioning used by teachers and students

The Common Core is pushing all teachers outside of their comfort zones, and will require teachers to regularly reflect upon their craft. This type of self-reflection/self-evaluation requires a high level of trust between the teachers on a team. If a team with a high level of trust does not exist in your building, video a lesson, invite an instructional coach and/or administrator to join you, and watch the lesson together using the look-fors mentioned above. This type of practice will allow for the necessary feedback that facilitates instructional change, and hopefully this practice will catch on with other teachers in the building.

Collaborative coaching is another powerful practice to support teacher collaboration. Collaborative coaching pairs allow teachers to observe each other in a nonevaluative manner, and learn from each other through observation. Teacher pairs meet together prior to observations to discuss what they want each other to observe and set times for the observations. The observing teacher looks for positive teacher and student behaviors ("wows") in the classroom and records as many as possible. For behaviors or strategies not observed, ask questions in the format of "I wonder if...." I suggest a ratio of three "wows" for every "I wonder if...." Teachers meet after the observation and discuss the notes and plan for the next observation. To make this beneficial and meaningful, consider personalities and teaching style to allow for growth. A teacher who believes direct instruction is the only way students learn could benefit from observing a classroom that uses cooperative learning strategies throughout the lesson, and a teacher who struggles with classroom management could observe a master teacher. Many teachers have shared that by observing others they glean new ideas for their classrooms and look forward to more opportunities of learning through the coaching pairs. Teaching is an isolated profession in many buildings, and the more collaboration and discussion around teaching practices is emphasized, the better teachers become at their craft.

PERSISTENCE LEADS TO SUCCESS

In order to be learners, both students and adults must never give up, and must realize that mistakes are OK and that learning from mistakes is the key to success. My students respect that I am a life-long learner and that I make mistakes regularly, but they know that I never give up. I use the following poem with both students and teachers when introducing new learning opportunities (Author unknown, from Bennett, 1993).

Try, Try Again
Tis a lesson you should heed,
Try, try again;
If at first you don't succeed,
Try, try again;
Then your courage should appear,
For, if you will persevere,
You will conquer, never fear;
Try, try again.

To create an engaging math class that everyone wants to be in, you must make engagement between the teacher, the students, and mathematics a priority. Thoughtfully creating opportunities that require students to engage in mathematical discourse through problem solving will force students to embody the mathematical practices and to grow as mathematicians. Sharing practices with fellow teachers through microstudy, lesson study, and collaborative coaching will continue to improve instruction and provide more rigorous learning opportunities for students.

I believe that all students can be successful, and I am excited about implementation of the Common Core content and practice standards. As the Common Core permeates your building and classrooms, keep in mind that these are exciting times to be in education and that we should be lifelong learners together, model the Common Core mathematical practice standards in all we say and do, and remember, if at first we don't succeed, to try, try again.

References

Ainsworth, L., & Christinson, J. (2011). *Five easy steps to a balanced math program training manual* (2nd ed.). Englewood, CO: Lead + Learn Press.

Ben-Hur, M. (2006). *Concept-rich mathematics instruction.* Alexandria, VA: Association for Supervision and Curriculum Development.

Bennett, W. J. (1993). *The book of virtues: A treasury of great moral stories.* New York, NY. Simon & Schuster.

Hattie, J. (2009). *Visible learning: A synthesis of over 800 meta-analyses relating to achievement.* New York, NY: Routledge.

Meyer, D. (2010). *Math class needs a makeover.* TED: Ideas Worth Spreading. Retrieved from http://www.ted.com/talks/dan_meyer _math_curriculum_makeover.html

National Council of Teachers of Mathematics. (2000). *Principles and standards for school mathematics.* Ann Arbor, MI: Authors.

National Governors Association Center for Best Practices & Council of Chief State School Officers (NGACBP & CCSSO). (2010). *Common core state standards.* Washington, DC: Authors.

National Research Council. (2001). *Adding it up: Helping children learn mathematics.* Washington DC: National Academies Press.

Stigler, J. W., & Hiebert, J. (1999). *The teaching gap: Best ideas from the world's teachers for improving education in the classroom.* New York, NY: The Free Press.

CHAPTER NINE

Balancing Science Instruction

Lynn Howard
and
Sharon Delesbore

"I love science! It's my favorite subject at school and my strongest. Science is a great example of life and people. It's also a great learning experience."

STUDENT

Ms. Bryd's second-grade classroom is abuzz with excitement. Each group of students has a variety of items, including a marble, a marshmallow, a cracker, a metal screw, and a raisin. They have completed the requirement of the science performance expectation—"Plan and conduct an investigation to describe and classify different kinds of materials by their observable properties"—and the science practice of planning and carrying out investigations. The "sink or float" assessment will allow them to demonstrate what they have learned. They have a lab response sheet to record their observations and for writing a summary statement. This experiment, applicable to all grade levels, is preparing students to participate in the science and engineering practices of the Next Generation Science Standards (NGSS) and the Common Core State Standards (CCSS).

DO YOU HAVE A BALANCED SCIENCE PROGRAM?

Ms. Bryd and science educators across the country are learning to "balance" their science programs through a process that integrates conceptual understanding of the standards; problem solving through research, demonstrations, and experiments; and best instructional practices. In addition to the Next Generation Science Standards, she is using Lynn Howard's *Five Easy Steps to a Balanced Science Program* (2010) to guide how she designs her science teaching and her students' learning. Her classroom has an atmosphere where students "do" science and are actively involved in learning the Big Ideas for each science unit.

The guiding questions in the pages that follow support implementation of a balanced approach to science instruction. The Next Generation Science Standards, conceptual understanding in science, and problem solving, used along with research-based educational strategies for all grades, provide a road map for effective science instruction that will impact teaching practices and student learning.

CURRENT STATE
OF SCIENCE STANDARDS

Are you prepared for the
Next Generation Science Standards?

The science standards and related documents presently used in many states and schools systems are about 15 years old. The National Academy of Sciences' *National Science Education Standards* were published in 1996, and the American Association for the Advancement of Science's *Benchmarks for Science Literacy* were published in 1993. With the development of the Common Core State Standards for literacy and math, science educators began the work to develop a common set of national standards for science, engineering, and technology. Students in the United States have consistently been outperformed on international tests and benchmarks such as the Trends in International Mathematics and Science Study (TIMSS) and the Program for International Student Assessment (PISA).

Conceptual Understanding

What do your students need to know
about science to function in today's world?

There is a basic understanding among scientists and science education experts that science instruction should promote meaningful understanding of science concepts, processes, and thoughts. The new standards movement is asking students to demonstrate a deep understanding of a few fundamental ideas (American Association for the Advancement of Science, 1993; National Academy of Sciences, 1996).

Science is an action. We "do" science. The authors of the Next Generation Science Standards decided to include "performance expectations" under the broad domains in each grade level. These clearly define what a student should know and be able to do upon completion of a grade level. A conceptual approach to learning science allows students to deepen scientific understanding by connecting science concepts to science meaning.

Ms. Koontz's fourth-grade English language learners are getting ready to conduct an experiment on energy. They will conduct research, observe demonstrations, and engage in experiments. The students have a problem-solving template and each group is ready to get started. Using a variety of common household materials, their task is to design three demonstrations that show their understanding of the performance expectation.

Ms. Koontz's students are focusing on this performance expectation: "Make observations to provide evidence that energy can be transferred from place to place by sound, light, heat, and electric current." The Big Idea for this unit is: "Energy can be transferred," and students will have multiple opportunities to understand the implication that this statement has on their own lives. Ms. Koontz has created a graphic organizer that indicates the skills and the content that her students must know and be able to do, as well as what level of rigorous thinking will be required. "Unwrapping" the performance expectations (see Figure 9.1) provides a clear understanding of what skills and concepts will be incorporated into the lesson, and the level of rigor of those skills and concepts.

	Concept/ Content	Bloom's Taxonomy Thinking Level	Webb's DOK Level
FIGURE 9.1 "Unwrapped" Skills and Concepts			
Skill	Concept/ Content	Bloom's Taxonomy Thinking Level	Webb's DOK Level
Make	Observations	Understanding (1)	Recall and Reproduction (1)
To Provide	Evidence (that waves transfer energy to objects)	Applying (3)	Strategic thinking and reasoning (3)

THE NEXT GENERATION SCIENCE STANDARDS

Have you explored the
Next Generation Science Standards document?

The Next Generation Science Standards were created based on *A Framework for K–12 Science Education* (2012), which was developed by the National Research Council (NRC). They were designed to guide our nation toward a scientifically literate society. Founded in exemplary practice and research, these standards describe a vision of the scientifically literate person. They describe what it means to be proficient in science, and present and explain the relationships between scientific and engineering practices, crosscutting concepts and disciplinary core ideas. In addition, the NGSS have been written to correlate with the depth of knowledge and rigor required by the Common Core ELA and math standards.

The Next Generation Science Standards are intended to reflect a new vision for American science education. The guiding principles are:

- K–12 science education should reflect the interconnected nature of science as it is practiced and experienced in the real world.

- The Next Generation Science Standards are student performance expectations—*not* curriculum.

- The science concepts in the NGSS build coherently from K to 12.

- The NGSS focus on deeper understanding of content as well as application of content.

- Science and engineering are integrated in the NGSS, from K to 12.

- The NGSS and Common Core State Standards (for both English language arts and mathematics) are aligned.

The understanding of science knowledge is not a linear path. Key components of research that have been supported by the National Science Teachers Association indicate that students must learn how to ask questions and use evidence to answer those questions. In the process of learning the strategies of scientific inquiry, students learn to conduct an investigation and collect evidence from a variety of sources, develop an explanation from the data, and communicate and defend their conclusions. The National Research Council's framework (which the NGSS are based on) describes what it means to be proficient for students in science in grades K–12. It supports science as a body of knowledge and an evidenced-based model that continually extends, refines, and re-vises science information. To successfully implement the NGSS, teachers will need to understand the importance and impact that the science and engineering practices will have on student learning. This will be a change in the way that science is delivered in the class-room. Students must be involved in talking about science content and concepts, applying problem-solving skills, and verifying and communicating their understandings, and they must be engaged with real-world experiences. The challenge is not just to read and implement the NGSS, but also to change the instructional environment in which students learn the standards.

The NRC framework for K–12 science education contains three dimensions (2012):

Dimension 1—
The Science and Engineering Practices

The science and engineering practices are based on be-haviors that scientists participate in as they investigate, explore, and explain models and theories about the natural world and the key engineering practices that are used to design and build models and systems. The NRC uses the term "practices" to emphasize that sci-entific investigation requires not only specific skills but also knowledge that is specific to each of the eight practices. By strengthening the engineering practices in the Next Generation Science Standards, students will have a clearer understanding of the relevance of science, technology, engineering, and mathematics (STEM) in relation to real-world experiences.

Dimension 2—
Crosscutting Concepts

The crosscutting concepts are the tool for linking the domains of science. They provide the organizational scheme for integrating knowledge from multiple science fields into a coherent and focused view of the scientifically based world. These concepts allow students to make connections in an integrated science world.

Dimension 3—
Disciplinary Core Ideas

The National Research Council defines disciplinary core ideas as "those that focus K–12 science curriculum, instruction, and assessments on the most important aspects of science disciplinary content knowledge."

SCIENCE LITERACY

Can your students read and understand scientific texts and proficiently communicate their information?

Science literacy is supported in *Five Easy Steps to a Balanced Science Program* (Howard, 2010) by aligning the Next Generation Science Standards with the Common Core English language arts and literacy standards. As school districts and schools address the need to improve reading across all grade levels, teachers are looking for strategies that can be used with science texts to improve reading, writing, and vocabulary acquisition. Teachers who are balancing their science program include best literacy practices as a major focus in all of their science units.

In order to be considered science literate in the 21st century, students must be able to do more than just recite facts and plug in formulas. According to the *National Science Education Standards* (National Academy of Sciences, 1996), "scientific literacy entails being able to read with understanding articles about science in the popular press and to engage in social conversation about the validity of the conclusions." In order for students to become scientifically literate, they must be given the opportunity to explore their interests and be curious about their world, to ask questions, to read for information, and to communicate their findings.

There is a natural connection between science and English language arts in that the standards define what it means to be a literate person in the 21st century. Students who meet the standards have the skills and understandings that are necessary for reading scientific writings or complex works of literature. They demonstrate the use of reasoning and use of evidence that supports collaboration and communication across all disciplines.

The practical applications of problem solving through research, demonstrations, and experiments signify the active participation of students in their learning of science. However, in the international world, literacy is no longer limited to reading. In this day and age, "knowledgeable" is the term that resonates with our efforts to develop a literate society in all core content areas, whether in science, English, math, or social studies. This makes understanding the Common Core State Standards in English Language Arts & Literacy in History/Social Studies, Science, and Technical Subjects even more imperative for all educators as we help students exemplify what it means to be science literate. The college and career readiness (CCR) anchor standards for reading and writing in the English language arts

CCSS bring a clear relevance to the instruction being required of our teachers and the learning being expected of our students.

The Common Core State Standards for ELA state: "The Standards insist that instruction in reading, writing, speaking, listening, and language be a shared responsibility within the school. The K–5 standards include expectations for reading, writing, speaking, listening, and language applicable to a range of subjects, including but not limited to ELA. The grades 6–12 standards are divided into two sections, one for ELA and the other for history/social studies, science, and technical subjects. This division reflects the unique, time-honored place of ELA teachers in developing students' literacy skills while at the same time recognizing that teachers in other areas must have a role in this development as well." It is suggested that science and English language arts teachers meet regularly to plan integrated reading and writing instructional lessons. Depending on grade level, science students will be asked to provide opinions or write arguments focused on specific content, develop problem-solving questions, determine evidence, and communicate their findings. All students will be involved in writing informative/explanatory texts, including historical events, scientific procedures/experiments, or technical processes. The organization and development of scientific topics, ideas, and concepts will lead to clear and coherent writing appropriate to the task, purpose, and audience. By the end of grade twelve, students will be required to write arguments to support claims in an analysis of topics or texts, using valid reasoning and sufficient evidence. In fact, the ELA standards lay the foundation for developing students' argumentative writing skills during the early grades, and it is stressed throughout the learning progressions. There is a natural link between argumentative writing and science.

PROBLEM SOLVING

How often do you integrate
problem solving in your classroom?

Problem solving, with experimentation, is the core of scientific exploration and investigation. Effective problem solving requires that students be presented with or identify a problem, follow a series of steps to a solution, and communicate their findings to others. The scientific method was recognized, developed, and used mainly by scientists, but many people do not recognize that it is a general process applicable to all areas of study. The scientific method has been the process by which scientists solve problems and conduct experiments for ages. In 1637, René Descartes published his *Discours de la Méthode* in which he described systematic rules for determining what is true, thereby establishing the principles of the scientific method. While there are no fixed steps that a scientist always follows, there is a concerted effort to provide a structured approach to problem solving.

The obvious truth that is not being addressed is that the educators from one content area cannot teach this method alone. It is a shared responsibility. By balancing research, demonstrations, and experiments through problem solving, teachers place emphasis on the knowledge and skills that reinforce science content and the increased demands of the Next Generation Science Standards.

Asking questions and defining problems is a unifying theme of the standards across all grade levels and content areas. It is the heart of scientific research, and guides everything that scientists and engineers do to improve the quality of life for all people. The science and engineering practices in the NGSS are derived from and grouped by the eight categories detailed in *A Framework for K–12*

Science Education (NRC, 2012). These are aligned with the Common Core mathematical practices, and are essential components in developing reasoning, advanced problem solving, critical and creative thinking, and constructing explanations (for science) and designing solutions (for engineering). Educators must intentionally provide students with opportunities to integrate both practices to foster student understanding. For example, the NGSS science and engineering practice of "asking questions and defining problems" directly aligns with the CCSS mathematical practice "make sense of problems and persevere in solving them." Science and math teachers have an opportunity to plan integrated instruction to include an alignment of these practices. A high school physics teacher focusing on "motion and stability: forces and interactions" could easily integrate this unit with a math teacher who is teaching about quadratic equations.

It is important to note that the purpose of these standards is to demonstrate the specific practice for which students will be held accountable—not to limit instruction. The NGSS science and engineering practices are not to be taught in isolation, but as an integral part of content instruction. Nonetheless, moving from the language of inquiry to that of science practices may require a shift for many science educators. It is suggested that teachers spend time learning and understanding the implications that both the science and math practices have on their classroom instruction.

The NGSS science and engineering practices are:

- Asking questions and defining problems
- Developing and using models
- Planning and carrying out investigations
- Analyzing and interpreting data

- Using mathematics, information, and computer technology
- Constructing explanations and designing solutions
- Engaging in argument from evidence
- Obtaining, evaluating, and communicating information

RESEARCH

How are your students like scientists?
Are your students practicing scientists?

An effective science classroom is one where the students are adopting the roles of scientists. Research is an essential key element in such an environment. When engaged in research, students are able to utilize science inquiry skills that are essential practices conducted by scientists. Scientific inquiry refers to "the diverse ways in which scientists study the natural world and propose explanations based on the evidence derived from their work. Scientific inquiry also refers to the activities through which students develop knowledge and understanding of scientific ideas, as well as an understanding of how scientists study the natural world," as defined by the *National Science Education Standards* (National Academy of Sciences, 1996, p. 23). The methods that scientists—and students— use to conduct scientific inquiry are called science process skills. The National Association for Research in Science Teaching helps to define the skills that students are expected to achieve in order to be globally competitive (Padilla, 1990).

Basic Science Process Skills

Observing: Using the senses to gather information about an object or event. Example: Describing a pencil as yellow.

Inferring: Making an "educated guess" about an object or event based on previously gathered data or information. Example: Saying that the person who used a pencil made a lot of mistakes because the eraser was well worn.

Measuring: Using both standard and nonstandard measures or estimates to describe the dimensions of an object or event. Example: Using a meter stick to measure the length of a table in centimeters.

Communicating: Using words or graphic symbols to describe an action, object, or event. Example: Describing the change in height of a plant over time in writing or through a graph.

Classifying: Grouping or ordering objects or events into categories based on properties or criteria. Example: Placing all rocks having a certain grain size or hardness into one group.

Predicting: Stating the expected outcome of a future event based on a pattern of evidence. Example: Predicting the height of a plant in two weeks' time based on a graph of its growth during the previous four weeks.

Integrated Science Process Skills

Controlling variables: Being able to identify variables that can affect an experimental outcome, and keeping most constant while manipulating only the independent variable. Example: Realizing through past experiences that the amount of light and water need to be controlled when testing to see how the addition of organic matter affects the growth of beans.

Defining operationally: Stating how to measure a variable in an experiment. Example: Stating that bean growth will be measured in centimeters per week.

Formulating hypotheses: Stating the expected outcome of an experiment. Example: The greater the amount of organic matter added to the soil, the greater the bean growth.

Interpreting data: Organizing data and drawing conclusions from it. Example: Recording data from the experiment on bean growth in a data table and forming a conclusion that relates trends in the data to variables.

Experimenting: Being able to conduct an experiment, including asking an appropriate question, stating a hypothesis, identifying and controlling variables, operationally defining those variables, designing a "fair" experiment, conducting the experiment, and interpreting the results of the experiment. Example: The entire process of conducting the experiment on the effect of organic matter on the growth of bean plants.

Formulating models: Creating a mental or physical model of a process or event. Example: Making a model of how the processes of evaporation and condensation interrelate in the water cycle.

In the Next Generation Science Standards, these skills have not been omitted or redefined, but rather amplified. The science process skills, which initially focused on the basics of observing, inferring, measuring, communicating, classifying, and predicting, have evolved into a second tier of scientific knowledge that consists of controlling variables, defining operationally, formulating hypotheses, interpreting data, experimenting, and formulating models.

DEMONSTRATION

How have you used demonstrations to support your teaching of science standards?

Another effective element to use in the science classroom is that of demonstration. Science demonstrations have the potential to establish an environment in which conversations about observations and the development of explanations can encourage students—especially those from urban schools who have not had many chances to do so—to engage in practices associated with science, such as observing, describing, talking, socially interacting, writing, problem solving, inquiring, testing, and explaining, as noted in the work of Milne and Otieno (2007). Recognize, though, that the essential characteristic of an effective demonstration is that it is *not* instructor-centered. The work of Majerich (2004), Majerich and Schmuckler (2006; 2007), and Majerich, Schmuckler, and Fadigan (2008) offers new insight into how to better prepare students to learn from demonstrations with a more student-centered science lecture demonstration method. By allowing students to participate in the inquiry process during demonstrations, the perception of science phenomenon, the learning of science topics, and the development of understandings about science can be achieved.

Majerich's work in 2004 identified a number of benefits associated with the teaching and learning of science using demonstrations:

- Demonstrations act as a motivational device, arouse curiosity, and gain students' attention.

- Demonstrations convey the instructor's attitude toward the discipline.

- Demonstrations stimulate the thought process of students (they challenge students' knowledge claims, naïve conceptions, and alternate conceptions).

- Demonstrations help students to focus and increase their attention.

- Demonstrations help students negotiate theory and experiments.

- Demonstrations help students see abstract science ideas in concrete examples.

- Demonstrations enhance students' learning of science concepts.

- Demonstrations serve as a substitute for laboratory exercises/experiments that are too costly or dangerous to students.

- Demonstrations develop creativity in students and promote cooperation among students/teachers.

Science demonstrations bring interaction and engagement to the science classroom; they alleviate the monotony and establish a different dynamic within the classroom. The use of science demonstrations can vary from making the abstract ideals of science become more concrete to introducing a discrepant event. A discrepant event is something that defies the "basic rules of science" (Howard, 2010). When demonstrating a discrepant event, teachers should identify the performance expectations for their grade level and expect students to provide solutions based on their prior experiences and content knowledge. For example, if you add 50 ml of water (H_2O) to 50 ml of alcohol (characterized by the OH group), you will find that you get a total volume of 97 ml rather than 100 ml. This is not what is expected, and the demonstration is now labeled as discrepant. Engagement and questioning strategies that propel the students to a higher level of thinking and intensify the rigor of the curriculum are positive outcomes of the use of demonstrations. Demonstrations can revitalize a science classroom.

EXPERIMENTATION

What are your successes and challenges with doing science experiments?

Mr. Sanders' high school physics class is beginning a unit called "extreme physics." The students are designing an experiment to study extrema, zeros, and other key values of quadratic functions in real-world scenarios. Their vocabulary includes velocity, distance, rate, speed, air resistance, and the quadratic equation. This activity is inspired by the annual Pumpkin Chunkin competition in Sussex County, Delaware, where the object is to throw a pumpkin, without totally destroying it, as far as possible from a homemade device. Although the actual competition uses hydraulic cannons and catapults, these students will be building and testing their own trebuchet. Two experiments will be completed. The first has students exploring equations that convert potential energy into kinetic energy. The second will have students finding the zeros, minimum or maximum, and y-intercept after launching and observing their own pumpkins. Students will be looking for answers to their hypotheses and drawing independent conclusions as they compare and analyze data with other groups.

Scientific inquiry is critical to the context of all science experiments. Most people think of an experiment as something that is done by scientists and takes place in a lab under special conditions. Although this is often true, some experiments can be conducted in places other than laboratories. An experiment is a test or investigation that is planned to provide evidence for or against a stated hypothesis. Usually involving research, experiments support scientific inquiry and problem solving. It is essential that best practices for experimentation be implemented on a regular basis in all K–12 science classrooms.

Science experiments do not need to be expensive or difficult. Teachers should carefully plan experiments so that the standards are supported and correlated to the established curriculum. The scientific method should be used to help students formulate the experiment and make conclusions about the activity. For example, kindergarten students who are practicing the science process skills might observe primary colors in frozen ice cubes that then melt to form secondary colors. Middle school students could use microscope slides and petroleum jelly to determine air quality in various locations in the school. And high school students could investigate erosional processes on a local stream and determine the impact that this would have over time in the community.

THE IMPACT ON THE
CLASSROOM TEACHER

What are your next steps
for refining your science teaching?

The Next Generation Science Standards stress that science is profoundly important in addressing the issues of the 21st century: "The purpose of science education, broadly expressed as STEM (Science, Technology, Engineering, and Mathematics) literacy, is to equip our students with the knowledge and skills essential for addressing society's needs. . . ." There must be a commitment to integrate engineering and technology into the structure of science education to the same level as scientific inquiry.

The teacher is the most important component in improving the quality of student learning. The best teachers are those who design classroom experiences that are of high interest, are motivating, and connect to real-world adventures in the lives of their students.

To successfully implement the NGSS, teachers will need to understand the importance and impact that the science and engineering practices will have on student learning. This will be a change in the way that science is delivered in the classroom. The research tells us how students learn science best and how to create an engaging classroom environment that leads to exploration and explanation of the natural world. Science best practices call for students to be involved in talking about science content and concepts, applying problem-solving skills, verifying and communicating their understandings, and engaging in real-world experiences. The challenge is not just to read and implement the NGSS, but also to change the instructional environment in which students learn the standards. The practices provide the outlines for this.

Our purpose for building scientifically literate students is simple: as educators, we want *all* students to be proficient in problem solving and higher-level thinking. We want them to be able to ask and find answers to questions arising from their own curiosity; explain and predict natural phenomena; read, understand, and be able to discuss articles about science in popular media; identify scientific issues underlying matters requiring national and local decisions; and use evidence and data to evaluate the quality of science information and arguments put forth by scientists and in the media. We must balance our instructional practices and increase the rigor of what we ask our students to learn in order to accomplish these things.

As you begin to implement the Next Generation Science Standards, take into consideration these suggestions:

- Talk about science in conversations and discussions on a daily basis.

- Allow for mistakes to be made. Start focusing on student misconceptions about science and provide evidence to support corrections.

- Have a high expectation that *all* students can learn and "do" science. Make connections with their real-world experiences.

- Learn to talk less and listen more to student conversations. Allow for more student discussion, interaction with the content, and inquiry learning.

- Do more problem solving. Allow students to use their own learning tools to investigate problems and arrive at solutions.

• Use cooperative and collaborative learning.

• Implement technology to collect, analyze, and interpret information, along with research and worldwide communication from other scientists.

A LINK TO THE FUTURE

The release of the Next Generation Science Standards comes at a time when most states are beginning to implement the Common Core State Standards in English language arts and math. The Next Generation Science Standards provide a vision of science teaching and learning that presents opportunities for *all* students to learn science. The NGSS' alignment to the CCSS ensures that all students have a comprehensive education built coherently on content and skills that are meaningful in real-world application. These new standards occur as the population in our nation becomes more diverse, and the substantial shifts in teaching science that will be necessary to implement the NGSS will be consistent with those needed to implement the ELA and mathematics CCSS. Science is critical in the lives of all Americans as they prepare to be informed citizens, compete in a global economy, and develop 21st-century skills in communication, collaboration, and critical and creative thinking. The NGSS, aligned with the CCSS, provide the necessary link to enable science educators to develop and sustain a balanced science program in their schools that teaches *all* students to be capable, exacting, discerning "scientists."

References

Achieve (on behalf of 26 states and partners that collaborated). (2013). *Next generation science standards*. Retrieved from http://www.nextgenscience.org/next-generation-science-standards

American Association for the Advancement of Science. (1993). *Benchmarks for science literacy*. New York, NY: Oxford University Press.

Howard, L. (2010). *Five easy steps to a balanced science program* (primary, upper elementary and middle school, and secondary volumes). Englewood: CO: Lead + Learn Press.

Majerich, D. M. (2004). *Developing understandings of chemistry in a large-enrollment science lecture demonstration-based course for non-majors: The extent of meaningful learning and implications for practice* (Doctoral dissertation, Temple University).

Majerich, D. M., & Schmuckler, J. S. (2006). *Compendium of demonstration-related research from 1918 to 2001*. Retrieved from www.drs.scienceinstruction.org/compendium_v1.doc

Majerich, D. M., & Schmuckler, J. S. (2007, May/June). Improving students' perceptions of benefits of science demonstrations and content mastery in a large-enrollment chemistry lecture demonstration course for nonscience majors. *The Journal of College Science Teaching. 36*(6), 60–67.

Majerich, D. M., Schmuckler, J. S., & Fadigan, K. (2008). *Compendium of science demonstration-related research from 1918 to 2008*. Philadelphia, PA: Xlibris.

Milne, C., & Otieno, T. (2007, July). Understanding engagement: Science demonstrations and emotional energy. *Science Education, 91*(4), 523–553.

National Academy of Sciences. (1996). *National science education standards.* Washington, DC: National Academies Press.

National Governors Association Center for Best Practices & Council of Chief State School Officers. (2010). *Common core state standards.* Washington, DC: Authors.

National Research Council. (2012). *A framework for K–12 science education: Practices, crosscutting concepts, and core ideas.* Washington, DC: National Academies Press.

Padilla, M. (1990). The science process skills. *Research matters—to the science teacher, no. 9004.* National Association for Research in Science Teaching. Retrieved from http://www.narst.org/publications/research/skill.cfm

PART THREE

Strategies for Specialized Situations

CHAPTER TEN

Re-Envisioning How We Teach English Language Learners

Rachel Syrja

"ELLs are a heterogeneous group with differences in ethnic background, first language, socioeconomic status, quality of prior schooling, and levels of English language proficiency. Effectively educating these students requires diagnosing each student instructionally, adjusting instruction accordingly, and closely monitoring student progress."

**NATIONAL GOVERNORS ASSOCIATION CENTER
FOR BEST PRACTICES and COUNCIL OF
CHIEF STATE SCHOOL OFFICERS, 2012, p.1**

The biggest question facing teachers of English language learners (ELLs) today is, "How will instruction look different for ELLs in the era of the Common Core standards?" While the Common Core State Standards (CCSS) movement has provided the impetus for schools and districts across the country to revisit their curriculum—"what" we teach—it should also challenge us to turn the spotlight on ourselves and illuminate instruction—"how" we teach. What we do, this sacred craft we call teaching, is complicated and challenging on a good day. Throw in the fact that most teachers are facing the most diverse classrooms they have ever had, with every type of learner from gifted to ELL, either "drizzled" or "poured" into every class, and we quite literally have a recipe for burnout and frustration. ELLs as a population are diverse, and therefore require that we develop lessons that reflect that diversity. While we hear this over and over again, the hard part is actually doing it.

The following pages will provide some guidance for teachers for dealing with diverse classrooms, and doing it well. A survey of demographic trends and the current state of instruction for ELLs, followed by a quick look at the absolute basics of working with English language learners, beginning with knowing and understanding students' language proficiency levels and continuing with a quick review of the basics of acquiring a second language, is a good place to start. It is also important to explore the importance of addressing the five domains—listening, speaking, reading, writing, and thinking—in every lesson we teach, along with the benefits of "unwrapping" the Common Core standards in order to clearly identify both the content and language objectives and communicate those objectives to our students.

In my role as a professional developer and instructional coach, I have the unique opportunity to visit schools and classrooms all across the nation, reinforcing teacher collaboration and working with teams to maximize their collaborative efforts. While research continues into what works for ELLs, what we currently know is that learning increases when teachers work *collaboratively* to incorporate high-impact strategies such as peer interaction, visuals, hands-on experiences, prereading activities, and scaffolded writing assignments (Echevarría, Vogt, and Short, 2010a). According to the Center for Research on the Educational Achievement and Teaching of English Language Learners (CREATE), in the upper grades, this collaborative work should also include designing lessons that develop vocabulary, academic language, and reading comprehension skills all within the context of content-area instruction (CREATE, 2012). Sadly, it never ceases to amaze me just how many of us insist on continuing to work in isolation, failing to realize the benefits of collaboration. A protocol for teacher collaboration will help to ensure that we are using strategies effectively and, more importantly, that we are pausing to evaluate the effectiveness of the strategies we use with our ELLs.

DEMOGRAPHIC TRENDS AND THE CURRENT STATE OF EDUCATION FOR ENGLISH LANGUAGE LEARNERS

It has been a well-established and widely accepted fact that English language learners lag far behind their native English-speaking peers in U.S. schools (National Center for Education Statistics, 2011). Considering the current state of instruction for ELLs, which confirms time and again that native English speakers continue to outperform ELLs on measures such as the NAEP (National Assessment of Educational Progress), it is imperative that we not just consider how ELLs will reach the same level of proficiency as their native English counterparts; because the achievement gap is so wide, we must consider how we will accelerate achievement for ELLs significantly over the course of the next few years.

The populations of elementary and secondary schools across

the United States continue to change as a result of record high numbers of immigrants entering the country. Between 1970 and 2000, the number of school-age children of immigrants grew from 6 percent to 19 percent (Ruiz-de-Velasco and Fix, 2000). The number of immigrant, migrant, and refugee students in the United States who have limited English proficiency is growing exponentially. In fact, students who are learning English as a second language are the fastest-growing segment of the school-age population. Along with a growing number of immigrants, the population of ELLs has also grown dramatically in the last 20 years. Between the years 1993 and 2003, the ELL population grew by 84 percent while the overall student population rose 12 percent. The number of ELLs in elementary schools from 1980 to 2000 increased from 5 to 7 percent, while in secondary schools the number of ELLs increased from 3 to 5 percent. After English, Spanish is the most widely used language currently spoken in the United States. It is estimated that approximately 20 percent of the school-age population speaks a language other than English: 14–16 percent speak Spanish as their primary language at home (Reyes and Moll, 2004); the rest of these children speak a language other than Spanish. When we consider the K–5 population of English language learners, we find that the majority, 76 percent, speak Spanish and are of Latino/Hispanic background (Capps, et al., 2004).

The data show that ELLs are highly concentrated in a few urban schools that are also highly minority, low income, and disproportionately likely to fail federal standards (Fix and Capps, 2005). In areas that are newly experiencing an influx of ELLs, the burden on schools is often overwhelming, as they often lack the resources and properly credentialed teachers to meet the needs of so many students. These demographic trends, coupled with the increased rigor of the CCSS, have led to a true crisis in educating ELLs. More than ever, it is imperative that teachers of English learners arm themselves with strategies that will help to ensure the success of their students.

THE BASICS OF ACQUIRING A SECOND LANGUAGE

English language learners have very specific needs, and those needs change depending on several factors, including:

Primary language proficiency: A student's proficiency level in their primary language has been shown to be a predictor of success in acquiring a second language. If a child arrives in our schools with a solid foundation—a high level of proficiency and literacy in their primary language—then development of the second language will be greatly facilitated (Collier and Thomas, 1989)

Stability: A student's language acquisition is negatively affected if they have a high rate of transiency during their educational career.

Maintenance of the native language: Students who maintain their native language are actually likely to outperform their native English-speaking peers (Cummins, 2000).

Prior schooling: If the ELL has had previous educational experience, then success in our school system becomes a matter of acclimation, because skills learned in their native country can be transferred.

Factors such as these greatly impact the learning needs of the individual ELL. The fact that ELL experiences can vary so broadly from population to population demands that our instruction be responsive to those variances. It requires not only that we deeply implement high-impact strategies, but also that we appropriately differentiate those strategies based on the very specific needs of each ELL.

How Long Does It Take to Acquire English?

The rate at which a child acquires a second language is dependent upon several factors, with the most influential factor being the amount of formal schooling the child had in their primary language. The most comprehensive study we have is a longitudinal study conducted by Wayne Thomas and Virginia Collier from 1982 and 1996. In that study, Thomas and Collier looked at the language acquisition of 700,000 students. They considered factors ranging from socioeconomic status to number of years of schooling in the primary language. Of all the factors considered, not surprisingly it is the amount of formal schooling prior to arriving in U.S. schools that outweighed all other variables (p. 14). Other noteworthy findings from their studies include the following (Thomas and Collier, 1997):

- Students between the ages of 8 and 11 who had 2–3 years of formal schooling in their native language took 5–7 years to test at grade level in English.

- Conversely, students with little or no formal schooling in their native language who arrived before the age of 8 took 7–10 years to test at grade level in English.

- Students who were below grade level in their native language took 7–10 years to reach just the 50th percentile, and many of them never reached grade-level proficiency.

While these data shed light on the amount of time it may take ELLs to reach proficiency on external tests, more pertinent to everyday classroom instruction is the research conducted by James Cummins, which found that a significant level of fluency in conversational language, or basic interpersonal communication skills (BICS), can be achieved in 2–3 years. However, academic language, or cognitive academic language proficiency (CALP), required between 5 and 7 years to attain near-native proficiency levels (Cummins, 1996). It is not difficult to see how BICS would develop first, since it is the social dimension of language that demonstrates a student's ability to converse in social settings with teachers and peers. Because it is a very concrete aspect of language, it takes less time to demonstrate near-native proficiency with BICS. On the other hand, CALP is the more abstract dimension of language that includes being able to read, write, and perform within a content-area classroom at grade level, and thus takes longer to develop. Sometimes, it is assumed that proficiency in BICS is equated with performance in CALP; however, we must keep in mind that oral production in English does not always equate with academic production in English. Too many ELLs "slip through the cracks" because they sound so proficient when we observe them in conversations with their peers or when speaking to us. The fact that humans are social creatures by nature ensures that students will develop BICS quite naturally and rapidly. The focus of our instruction every day until students are reclassified to English proficient status should be the development of CALP. We need to keep this at the forefront of every instructional decision we make in our classrooms. The guiding question of every lesson we teach should be: "How does this lesson/activity develop cognitive academic language proficiency for my English learners?"

EFFECTIVE INSTRUCTION FOR ENGLISH LANGUAGE LEARNERS

Effective instruction for English learners provides access to the core curriculum and, at the same time, intentionally develops English language proficiency. Specific features of high-quality instruction include explicitly teaching the academic language required to complete the lesson's activities and assignments, activating and strengthening students' background knowledge, promoting oral interaction and extended academic talk, and reviewing vocabulary and content concepts to provide repetition of key ideas and their associated language (Echevarria and Short, 2009). Clearly all of these strategies build a student's academic language, thus facilitating the development of CALP.

Who Is Responsible for Developing English Language Proficiency?

It is important to identify to which teacher this responsibility falls. Many districts dole out the teaching of English language development (ELD) to specially credentialed teachers and their paraprofessionals. Unfortunately, while this is not an uncommon model, it is increasingly unusual to find schools with this model in place, and in which all teachers, from the ELD teacher to the self-contained or regular education teachers, take responsibility for the language proficiency of each English learner in their classrooms, whether that be one student or 30. It therefore bears stating that it is not solely the responsibility of these specialized teachers to get our ELLs to proficiency in English. In many schools, these specialists only see their students for 30–45 minutes per day. That leaves the majority of the school day to another teacher or teachers. All teachers of English learners must share the responsibility of fully educating them. In an era of ever-increasing academic demands, we can no longer afford to assume that someone else is responsible for doing what all of us will ultimately be held accountable for.

LANGUAGE PROFICIENCY LEVELS

Demographic trends as well as research into what works with English learners should send a loud and clear message to teachers who work with ELLs that we not only need to ensure that we are identifying and using the most effective strategies but also need to deeply implement those strategies. Even more importantly, we need to differentiate those strategies to meet the very diverse needs of the students we are working with. In order to effectively differentiate instruction, we must know and understand the language proficiency levels of the English learners we teach.

For all schools with English learners, it is important to take the time to ensure that every educator who comes in contact with ELLs is aware of the different stages of language acquisition. Knowing and understanding the levels of language acquisition helps all teachers identify appropriate strategies to use with ELLs. ELD teachers may have vast knowledge about language acquisition levels; however, regular classroom teachers who may encounter ELLs during their content-area instruction benefit greatly from understanding these levels as well. The following list adapted from the work of Krashen and Terrel (1983) contains a robust description of each language acquisition level, including the approximate length of time required to achieve it.

Level 1: Pre-Production (0–6 months)

- Speaks in single words
- May respond with 2- to 3-word phrases
- Has a very limited vocabulary, mostly basic interpersonal communication skills (BICS)
- Uses drawings to communicate thoughts and ideas
- Points or gestures to communicate basic needs
- Dependent on native language

Level 2: Early Production (6 months to 1 year)

- Speaks in short phrases and fragments
- Begins to use short, simple sentences
- May point or gesture to communicate preferences (Do you want a hamburger or hot dog?)
- Has a limited but basic vocabulary consisting mostly of BICS
- Errors in grammar may hamper meaning
- Uses familiar words and phrases

Level 3: Speech Emergence (1–3 years)

- Speaks using simple, uncomplicated sentences

- Begins to vary sentence structure
- Uses appropriate grammar and word order, but errors are still common
- Uses present or past tense only
- Errors may still hamper meaning
- Begins to use basic academic knowledge from content areas, or Cognitive Academic Language Proficiency (CALP)
- Emerging fluency

Level 4: Intermediate Fluency (3–5 years)

- Uses complete sentences
- Uses varied sentence structure
- Uses a range of vocabulary sufficient to express ideas
- Uses appropriate word order and grammar, but may make minor errors
- Begins to experiment with more complex verb forms
- Errors rarely interfere with communication
- Often requires rereading for meaning
- Uses academic vocabulary
- Able to use details when retelling or relating personal stories
- Improved narrative writing

Level 5: Advanced Fluency (5–7 years)

- Writes complete sentences

- Writes narratives
- Uses complex verb forms
- Uses varied and complex sentence structure
- Has a broad social and academic vocabulary
- Uses grammar and word order approximating that of a native speaker
- Errors no longer interfere with communication
- Has grade-level appropriate fluency approximating that of a native speaker
- Reads for meaning
- Correctly uses academic language

According to Title III legislation, all ELLs are required to be assessed once a year to determine language proficiency levels and assess progress in acquiring English, but it is also critical that schools and districts develop a language proficiency assessment tool of their own that helps teachers track the language development of every language learner periodically throughout the course of the year. Developing differentiated common formative assessments (CFAs) is critical to designing instruction as well as determining the effectiveness of the strategies that we are using. More importantly, it helps us identify those practices that are not working and that we need to cease using or modify. The *Common Formative Assessments for English Language Learners* seminar, based upon the book by the same title (Syrja, 2012), offers a step-by-step process for developing these assessments. Appropriately differentiating CFAs ensures that we are able to be responsive to the needs of our ELLs and design instruction that is not just appropriate to their level but also helps propel their learning forward to the next level of language acquisition.

Armed with this information, all teachers of English learners are able to design differentiated lessons that meet the ever-changing needs of their students. Using information such as that provided in the list of language acquisition level descriptions or in the "can-do descriptors" on the World-Class Instructional Design and Assessment Web site (WIDA, 2012), teachers can take existing lessons and ensure that they are strategically teaching their ELLs the skills they need to be successful in their current level of language acquisition, which helps to set the foundation for the next level of language acquisition. Only in this way will we prevent English learners from remaining "stuck" or "fossilized" at language proficiency level 3 for years to come (Bishop, 2010; Syrja, 2011).

TEACHING WITH THE FIVE DOMAINS IN MIND

For English language learners, engaging the five domains—listening, speaking, reading, writing, and thinking—as much as possible throughout the course of the instructional day is imperative and cannot be overlooked. It is important to keep in mind that while English learners will be more dependent upon the domain of listening in the beginning, that does not mean that we should exclude them from opportunities to engage in the other domains of language whenever they feel ready to do so. In fact, English learners should have opportunities every day to engage in the five domains. As you plan instruction, particularly for level 1 and 2 English learners, ensure that you are not excluding them from any of the other domains of language. Some great strategies for supporting English learners in the early levels of language acquisition without overwhelming them or raising their anxiety levels include using sentence starters in speaking and writing. In fact, the walls of our classrooms should be covered in language that students can use. But also remember that the idea is to provide support in the event that a student feels ready, but at the same time we must remember that English learners should have the right to remain silent until they feel ready (Asher, 2009).

"UNWRAPPING" THE STANDARDS TO IDENTIFY CONTENT AND LANGUAGE OBJECTIVES

How can we ensure that we don't repeat the same mistakes of the initial standards movement? This has been a question that many respected researchers have grappled with. Each warns that we must do things differently this time. We cannot continue using the same practices and expecting different results. While the standards documents of the 1990s varied widely in specificity and quality, what destined them for failure was the fact that in many cases, classroom teaching and assessment remained indistinguishable from the pre-standards era (Reeves, et al., 2011). The CCSS will only make a difference for our English learners and all students if we take this opportunity to truly change the trajectory of their educational experience. They can no longer afford to sit unchallenged and unmotivated in countless classrooms across the country and be expected to be successful if we do not provide them with the knowledge and skills they require and, in fact, deserve. The Common Core standards represent a direct response to the problem of instruction and curriculum that have become increasingly formulaic and textbook-driven, curriculum that is "a mile wide and an inch deep." These standards are a substantial answer to that challenge. Rather than continuing our march through textbooks convincing ourselves that they and they alone hold the key to learning for our students, we need to become truly standards-driven. That begins with a process that Larry Ainsworth calls "unwrapping" the standards (Ainsworth, 2003). It is through this process of breaking the standards down into their component concepts and skills and identifying the corresponding level of rigor of the standards that we can truly identify the learning expectations for our students.

"Unwrapping" the standards refers to a process by which the concepts (nouns) and skills (verbs) that all students should know and be able to do are identified for a unit of instruction and its corresponding assessment. Content or self-contained mainstream teachers will focus on "unwrapping" the prioritized CCSS content standards, while ELD teachers will "unwrap" the pertinent language proficiency standards that align with their units of instruction. This "unwrapping" process will also help us to intentionally align and differentiate our common formative assessments.

Once the nouns (concepts) and verbs (skills) have been identified, teams of teachers should work collaboratively to identify the level of rigor of the standard by using both Bloom's Taxonomy and Webb's Depth of Knowledge (DOK). In Figure 10.1, a Common Core standard has been "unwrapped" into its component parts.

The "unwrapped" standards can assist teams of teachers in developing the content and language objectives of their lessons. According to Echevarria, Vogt, and Short (2010b), content objectives identify what students will learn and be able to do in the lesson, and language objectives address the aspects of academic language that will be developed or reinforced. Research suggests

FIGURE 10.1	Example of "Unwrapping" a Standard

Standard 4.G.2: Classify two-dimensional figures based on the presence or absence of parallel or perpendicular lines, or the presence or absence of angles of a specified size. Recognize right triangles as a category, and identify right triangles.

Skills	Concepts	Bloom's	DOK
Classify	Two-dimensional figures	3	2
Recognize	Right triangles	1	1
Identify	Right triangles	1	1

that objectives should be stated in clear and simple language and posted in the classroom for the students to see. Furthermore, they should be read aloud at the beginning of the lesson so that students understand the lesson's purpose, and they should again be reviewed at the end of the lesson to determine whether the objectives were met. While content objectives have become second nature for many teachers, most of us struggle with developing language objectives to accompany the content objectives. Here are some suggestions (Himmel, Short, Richards, and Echevarria, 2012):

- Decide the key vocabulary, academic vocabulary, and other concept words that students may need in order to be able to speak, read, and write about the lesson.

- Consider the language skills that students will require in order to be able to carry out the tasks in the lesson.

- Identify the language and grammar structures common to the content area. For example, textbooks use comparative language structures to analyze two related concepts.

- Consider the tasks that the students will complete in the lesson and the language that will be embedded in those assignments.

Let's consider an example using the standard in Figure 10.1 as the basis for our content objective.

Language Objective: Students will be able to orally classify two-dimensional figures. Students will be able to orally identify right triangles.

Content Objective: Students will be able to produce a visual representation of two-dimensional figures. Given a set of triangles, students will be able to sort right triangles from nonright triangles.

The most important element to keep in mind when writing our objectives is that they need to be measurable. One way to ensure this is to use appropriate action verbs such as (adapted from CREATE, 2012):

Sample Content Objective Verbs: Apply, categorize, calculate, design, identify, select, create, hypothesize, use, solve.

Sample Language Objective Verbs: Compose, scan, discuss, read, list, persuade, state, record, listen, compare.

We should always keep in mind that students at the lowest levels of language proficiency can be challenged at the highest levels of Bloom's taxonomy and Webb's Depth of Knowledge (Syrja, 2011).

If we are to succeed at helping our students develop the necessary CALP required for them to be successful, then we must identify both the content and language objectives for every CCSS-based lesson we teach.

TEACHER COLLABORATION

As stated in numerous resources, the new Common Core State Standards are not a curriculum. They are a clear set of shared goals and expectations for the knowledge and skills that will help our students succeed. Local teachers, principals, superintendents, and others will decide *how* the standards are to be met. Teachers will continue to devise lesson plans and tailor instruction to the individual needs of the students in their classrooms. They will continue to consider the gamut of student needs and design lessons that meet the needs of those students. How does that differ from what we've been doing? Along with these new standards, research on what students require to be prepared for the workforce in the 21st century points to a world and set of skills unlike the world my generation prepared for so many years ago. This will require teachers to work collaboratively to share strategies like never before.

After spending the last five years coaching teachers in the classroom, it is clear to me that the best understanding of what works in classrooms comes from the teachers who are in them. That's why the standards establish *what* students need to learn, but do not dictate *how* teachers should teach. Instead, schools and teachers will decide how best to help students reach the standard. One of the most proven strategies for identifying what works with diverse populations of students is the Data Teams process. This research-proven collaboration protocol consists of the following steps:

1. Collect and chart data

2. Analyze data and prioritize needs

3. Set, review, and revise incremental SMART goals (specific, measurable, attainable, relevant, timely)

4. Select instructional strategies

5. Determine results indicators

6. Monitor and evaluate results

This proven process ensures that teachers work collaboratively not just to identify strategies, but also to determine which strategies are having the greatest impact on student achievement. It is these very strategies that we need to replicate in order to close the achievement gap for ELLs.

CLOSING THE GAP

While the achievement gap continues to persist between English learners and their native English-speaking peers, the CCSS have provided us with a new opportunity to rededicate ourselves to changing the trajectory for them dramatically. By ensuring that every teacher who works with ELLs is aware of and understands the language proficiency levels, we can pave the way for making sure that lessons are being differentiated appropriately for each level of language acquisition. By developing lessons that engage all five language domains—listening, speaking, reading, writing, and thinking—we can guarantee that students will be actively engaged in learning, as they should be. We can "unwrap" the Common Core standards to help us identify the language and content objectives for our ELLs and utilize the Data Teams process to help us identify and replicate best practices. It is only through the use of such research-based strategies that we will ever truly close the achievement gap.

References

Ainsworth, L. (2003). *"Unwrapping" the standards.* Englewood, CO: Advanced Learning Press.

Asher, J. J. (2009). The total physical response: Review of the evidence. *Total Physical Response World.* Retrieved from http://www.tpr-world.com/review_evidence.pdf

Bishop, B. (2010). *Accelerating academic achievement for English language learners* (seminar manual). Englewood, CO: Lead + Learn Press.

Capps, R., Fix, M., Ost, J., Reardon-Anderson, J., & Passel, J. (2004). *The health and well-being of young children of immigrants.* New York, NY: Urban Institute.

Center for Research on the Educational Achievement and Teaching of English Language Learners (CREATE). (2012). *Improving educational outcomes for English learners in the middle grades: The CREATE briefs collection.* Washington, DC: Center for Applied Linguistics.

Collier, V. P., & Thomas, W. P. (1989). How quickly can immigrants become proficient in school English? *Journal of Educational Issues of Language Minority Students, 5,* 26–38.

Cummins, J. (1996). *Negotiating identities: Education for empowerment in a diverse society.* Los Angeles, CA: California Association for Bilingual Education.

Cummins, J. (2000). *Language, power, and pedagogy: Bilingual children in the crossfire.* Clevedon, UK: Multilingual Matters.

Echevarria, J., & Short, D. (2009). Programs and practices for effective sheltered content instruction. In D. Dolson & L. Burnham-Massey (Eds.), *Improving education for English learners: Research-based approaches.* Sacramento, CA: California Department of Education Press.

Echevarria, J., Vogt, M., & Short, D. (2010a). *Making content comprehensible for secondary English learners: The SIOP Model.* Boston, MA: Allyn & Bacon.

Echevarria, J., Vogt, M. E., & Short, D. (2010b). *The SIOP model for teaching mathematics to English learners.* Needham Heights, MA: Allyn & Bacon.

Fix, M. E., & Capps, R. (2005). *Immigrant children, urban schools, and the No Child Left Behind Act.* Washington, DC: Migration Policy Institute. Retrieved March 26, 2013, from http://www.migrationinformation.org/usfocus/display.cfm?ID=347

Himmel, J., Short, D., Richards, C., and Echevarria, J. (2012). *Using the SIOP model to improve middle school science instruction: The CREATE briefs collection.* Washington, DC: Center for Applied Linguistics.

Krashen, S. D., & Terrell, T. D. (1983). *The natural approach: Language acquisition in the classroom.* Oxford, UK: Pergamon.

National Center for Education Statistics. (2011). *National Assessment of Educational Progress (NAEP) 2011 assessment.* Washington, DC: U.S. Department of Education.

National Governors Association Center for Best Practices & Council of Chief State School Officers. (2012). Application of common core state standards for English language learners. *Common core state standards.* Washington, DC: Authors. Retrieved from http://www.corestandards.org/assets/application-for-english -learners.pdf

Reeves, D., Wiggs, M., Lassiter, C., Piercy, T., Ventura, S., & Bell, B. (2011). *Navigating implementation of the common core state standards.* Englewood, CO: Lead + Learn Press.

Reyes, I., & Moll, L. (2004). Latinos and bilingualism. In *Encyclopedia Latina.* New York, NY: Grolier.

Ruiz-de-Velasco, J., & Fix, M. E. (2000). *Overlooked and underserved: Immigrant students in U.S. secondary schools.* Washington, DC: Urban Institute Press.

Syrja, R. (2011). *How to reach and teach English language learners: Practical strategies to ensure success for English language learners.* San Francisco, CA: Jossey-Bass.

Syrja, R. (2012). *Common formative assessments for English language learners.* Englewood, CO: Lead + Learn Press.

Thomas, W.P., & Collier, V. P. (1997, December). School effectiveness for language minority students. *National Clearinghouse for English Language Acquisition (NCELA) Resource Collection Series, 9.* Retrieved from http://www.thomasandcollier.com/ Downloads/1997_Thomas-Collier97.pdf

World-Class Instructional Design and Assessment (WIDA). (2012). *WIDA's can-do descriptors.* Retrieved from http://www.wida.us/ standards/CAN_DOs/

CHAPTER ELEVEN

RTI in the Common Core Era

Thomas Hierck

In the introduction to their book *Pyramid of Behavior Interventions: Seven Keys to a Positive Learning Environment* (2011, p. 1), Hierck, Coleman, and Weber suggest: "Education has changed. The job we are asked to do today is not the same job we were asked to do a decade ago. The focus has changed from *learning for some* to *learning for all*, and then to *learning for all, whatever it takes.* The stakes are higher than ever before."

The authors were not even considering the advent of the Common Core State Standards when they crafted those words. Imagine, then, how high the stakes have become with this additional set of expectations. How districts, schools, and individual teachers bridge the gap between current practice and the desired outcomes to ensure learning for *all*, whatever it takes, is the challenge before us. Response to Intervention (RTI) offers a practical approach to meeting that challenge. Moreover, the attributes that schools must ensure that all students acquire to graduate ready for college or a skilled career extend beyond academics; the development of positive social and academic *behaviors* is equally vital.

It is critical to keep in mind that RTI structures address both the behavioral and the academic components of the efforts of students. As Buffum, Mattos, and Weber (2009) note, "Behavior and academic achievement are inextricably linked. A student's academic success in school is directly related to the student's attention, engagement, and behavior" (p. 111). As you examine the language of the CCSS, keep in mind that the intended audience for these standards is *all* students with the possible exception of the one percent of students with the most significant cognitive disabilities who may be in an adult care facility after completing their school requirements.

Within the expectations of the CCSS are numerous statements to indicate that all students should be held to the same high expectations. For example, "Supports and accommodations should ensure that students receive access to multiple means of learning and opportunities to demonstrate knowledge, but retain the rigor and high expectations of the Common Core State Standards" (National Governors Association Center for Best Practices and Council of Chief State School Officers, 2010). The CCSS also expects that educators should "provide additional time, appropriate instructional support, and aligned assessments as (ELLs) acquire both English language proficiency and content area knowledge" (NGACBP and CCSSO, 2010). This will compel all educators to consider what needs to look different from current practice in terms of addressing the needs of this growing population of students. It will require a shift away from the all too familiar practice of "sentencing students to special education," where they often remain for the rest of their school careers. A clear definition of intervention will need to be crafted as educators work with students to close existing gaps in learning, not exacerbate them by watering down the requirements for students.

To be clear, there are two equally crucial 21st-century challenges codified in the Common Core State Standards. First, all students must learn at the level of depth and complexity required of today's citizenry. Second, the rigor of the skills that students must master has never been greater. Notably, the Common Core State Standards anticipate that some students will require more time and alternative approaches. In other words, students will require RTI-based systems of support to meet this lofty, necessary level of success.

Further specific language in the CCSS outlines the things that must be available to students receiving special education services in order for them to demonstrate their conceptual and procedural knowledge and skills in English language arts and mathematics (NGACBP and CCSSO, 2010):

- Appropriate accommodations and supports as well as related services designed to meet the unique needs of these students and to enable their access to the general education curriculum with the expectation that they may transition to higher achievement based on demonstrated outcomes.

- An Individualized Education Plan (IEP) that includes annual goals aligned with, and chosen to facilitate their attainment of, grade-level academic standards (which will require teachers to understand how the standards fit together vertically and which standards align with a student's current status).

- Teachers and other specialized instructional support personnel who are prepared and qualified to deliver high-quality, evidence-based, individualized instruction and support services. This will demand an increased collaboration between teachers and other service providers as well as an overall increase in teacher knowledge as it relates to special education.

The standards do *not* define the following:

- The intervention methods or materials necessary to support students who are well below or well above grade-level expectations.
- The full range of supports appropriate for ELLs and students with special needs, though the standards stress that *all* students must have the opportunity to learn and meet the same high standards.

This transition will also create the expectation of an increase in general education teachers' knowledge regarding what constitutes a learning disability and how they might teach a student with this unique learning style. Fortunately, the basic tenets of Response to Intervention will provide avenues to assist teachers as they meet these expectations. Universal screening, progress monitoring, data-based decision making, and Tier 1, 2, and 3 interventions will facilitate the planning process and instructional design.

UNIVERSAL SCREENING

Universal screening can be simply defined as the process educators use to identify those students who might need more time and support to complete the expected academic or behavioral outcomes. There is no excuse for us to delay supports for students desperately at risk. If it's predictable, it's preventable. We can predict that students significantly behind their peers during a current school year are going to experience significant difficulties in the subsequent school year. The good news is that we can efficiently screen, using existing data, brief assessments, or even our collective professional knowledge, to identify these students. Once we gather these data, we can embed supports within these students' daily schedules on the very first day of school. Again, if it's predictable, it's preventable. We can prevent students from languishing at the beginning of the year while we organize ourselves. We can prevent our frustrations and surprise when these students fail to master, or even access, essential content.

The best universal screening assessments are valid, reliable, and demonstrate diagnostic accuracy in helping educators to plan out appropriate interventions. As the name implies, these assessments are conducted with all students to accurately pinpoint those who require this additional assistance. These diagnostic tools will need to be aligned with the new Common Core standards (and the new curriculum your school or district may design to further this alignment) to ensure fidelity. Schools and districts should also consider preparing for the reality of a drop in scores that may negatively impact those students already identified as struggling. For example, the state of Kentucky saw an immediate 30 to 40 point drop in proficiency when they rolled out new assessments aligned with the CCSS (Ujifusa, 2013). Current assessments may focus on basic skills assessment, while next generation assessments look at college and career readiness. Consideration will have to be given to those students already receiving intervention as to the impact these results may have on the level of services students receive and what needs to happen to maintain and improve those services.

PROGRESS MONITORING

Once students have been identified and are receiving the necessary interventions, their progress must be monitored, in order to both drive the instructional process and monitor the efficacy of the intervention. The simple question is, "Is it working?" The more difficult question is, "If it's not working, am I prepared to do something else?" In order to be effective, progress monitoring assessments need to be conducted at least bimonthly, with an eye toward identifying students who are not demonstrating acceptable progress and monitoring the effectiveness of various teaching strategies to identify those that lead to better student outcomes. Buffum, Mattos, and Weber (2012) suggest that progress monitoring is the one area of RTI they see schools struggle with more than any other component. They identify two reasons for this struggle (pp. 90–91):

> For many schools, the difficulty is not an assessment problem, but a targeting problem. Many schools offer only broad interventions: they place all students who are failing math into the same intervention, but because their needs are all different, the teacher in charge of the intervention is unsure how to monitor progress on those diverse needs. The second reason is because they create overly demanding, oppressive RTI documentation processes.

The progress monitoring checks must be aligned with the standards and with any new curricular elements that emerge as a result of their implementation. The expectations educators have for growth and the scores they use to determine this growth will also need to be aligned.

DATA-BASED DECISION MAKING

Data-based decision making ties in with progress monitoring, in that educators must focus on what types of screening, progress monitoring, and formative data to examine to determine the adequacy of the core instructional practices and curriculum. Additionally, these data are used to examine the effectiveness of the implemented behavioral strategies for the various groups of students. This examination of the data is best managed and monitored collaboratively during structured times set aside for professional learning communities and/or Data Teams. The group can determine if instruction needs to become more or less intensive. Schools will need to review the kinds of data they gather and how they will examine these data to ensure mastery of the essential skills *all* students need to comply with the Common Core. Decisions related to needs at the individual student, classroom, school, or district level will help to shape what supports are needed going forward. The Data Teams process developed by The Leadership and Learning Center enables educators to make data-driven decisions at the classroom level. Data Teams follow a specific step-by-step process to examine student work, apply effective instructional strategies including interventions, and monitor student learning in response to the strategies and interventions.

TIER 1 (CORE INSTRUCTION)

Tier 1 simply represents the research-based core curriculum and instructional practices used for all students. Tier 1 instruction must ensure access to differentiated learning activities that address individual needs, and scaffolds that provide students access to learning essential content and skills. Not "slower and louder," but actual adjustments that meet the learners at the level they are at on the learning progression continuum. These accommodations need to ensure that all students have access to the instructional program and should include structures to address behavior problems that have the potential to prevent students from demonstrating the academic skills they possess. Again, if it's predictable, it's preventable.

This tier is also the place where teachers design and provide enrichment activities for those students who either already have the prerequisite knowledge or who grasp the new concepts quickly: not "more of the same," but an attempt to enrich the learning experience and extend the thinking for these demonstrably able learners. The adoption of the CCSS will stretch teachers in differentiating and enriching, particularly when it comes to adequate resource support. It's not likely that a textbook will exist to meet these expectations, so much material will need to be created contextually to address the needs of the students in class today. Consideration will also need to be given to expanding the repertoire of general education teachers through professional development as they look to work with students who may have traditionally been referred out of their classrooms for support from special education practitioners.

To illustrate this first tier, let's look at a typical math lesson that involves solving a multistep problem. Keep in mind that one of the key developmental steps in effective problem solving is to provide students with opportunities to solve (and struggle with) problems, so differentiating is the key approach at Tier 1. This differentiation can be within the task (instead of between tasks) and could involve students differentiating themselves by identifying what parts of the problem they can and cannot perform with mastery. The teacher would then provide the additional support (but not the answer) the student needs to achieve mastery. Differentiation can also include the teacher presenting and the students interacting with the task through concrete, representational, and abstract examples. A concrete example may include three-dimensional algebra tiles, a representation example may include a visual, two-dimensional depiction of the algebra tiles, and an abstract example may involve variables and numbers.

TIER 2

Some students may require additional time and differentiated supports to master the essentials. Progress monitoring in the form of common formative assessments provides this information. Students can be grouped more homogeneously during this time, and they may receive support in a smaller group from the teacher who has had the most success, as measured by those common formative assessments. This is another place in the process where the information gathered during the Data Teams process can be put to use. Identifying the cause of the struggle an individual student, or a group of students, is experiencing allows for greater clarity in the potential intervention and, by extension, the impact of that intervention. Teachers need to be clear about the instructional procedures, duration, and frequency of instruction for the intervention. The Common Core may create a challenge here, as teachers wrestle with the notion of skill recovery versus skills to be achieved as outlined in the standards. Will timetable adjustments allow for additional time to be carved out addressing the deficits?

Continuing with the example in Tier 1, the strategies employed at Tier 2 would be driven by the identified gaps that could not be remediated by the initial differentiated instruction in Tier 1. This may involve modifying instruction (reteaching, identifying smaller learning progressions, visual representation) in solving multistep problems, or could involve structured peer-to-peer teaching. Teachers may provide an explicit review of the immediate prerequisite skills for solving two-step equations, such as operations with integers or the meaning of equality. At this tier, students would be placed in smaller groups (five to eight students) to receive some additional time or intensity on the areas they have been struggling with.

TIER 3

Tier 3 is the most intense of the three levels of intervention. These are the students with severe motivational issues, behavioral concerns, and irregular attendance patterns. This may also include students who are significantly behind in the core skills of English language arts and math, or who struggle with the English language. Intervention needs to be individualized to target each student's area(s) of need. Tier 3 supports may need to be provided, temporarily, in place of another important content area (other than literacy and mathematics). Schools may consider alternating what content a student misses from week to week while engaged in this intensive intervention. While this is not the most favorable of options, it is important to recognize that oftentimes students with individualized education programs or who ultimately drop out do not typically experience the rich options available to other student as they progress through school.

Another factor to keep in mind is that Tier 3 supports should not be rigidly designed to last 30 minutes, or be provided in groups with a specific student-teacher ratio, or be provided with a specific program. The support should be adjusted to match student needs and revised until the student is adequately responding to intervention. As Tier 3 students progress through the expectation of the Common Core, it will be imperative for their classroom teachers, special education teachers, and interventionists to have regular and frequent dialogue.

Continuing with the example of solving a multistep math problem, students identified as Tier 3 would receive similar additional time and intensity on the areas of struggle as with Tier 2, but with added frequency. Students may require support with foundational prerequisite skills, such as number sense or basic whole-number operations. This becomes an emergent need that requires immediate and intense intervention. The group size would be reduced (three to five students) or may even involve one-to-one instruction.

KEY INTERVENTION ELEMENTS

McNulty and Gloeckler (2011), in a white paper for the International Center for Leadership in Education, identified five key elements that schools must address to support the achievement of students receiving special education services. Their suggestions are adapted and listed here:

Ownership: Understanding among staff that students receiving special education services are the responsibility of all. Every student that crosses the threshold of your school is the responsibility of every adult that works there. This expectation extends beyond the assignment you may have individually.

High expectations: Understanding by administrators, faculty, and students that all students will be challenged and expected to perform to the best of their abilities. All means *all*. Any expectation less than this would be a dereliction of our duty and responsibility to improve the life chances of every child.

Intervention systems: Policies, procedures, and protocols to ensure that struggling learners meet academic and/or behavioral expectations as measured by improved performance. An "intervention" must be just that, and not a permanent condition imposed on a student.

Inclusion/Collaborative Teaching: Teaching methodologies in which students receiving special education services are included in the general education classrooms and have access to both content and special education expertise. Differentiation strategies and additional supports should not result in students being removed from core instruction, but instead should augment that instruction.

Organization/Professional Development: Successful programs for all struggling learners depend on alignment of, and access to, standards-based curriculum, instruction, and assessment, and data-driven professional development, to support teachers in achieving goals. Clarity precedes competence. All educators need fluency in what expectations there are and supports in helping to achieve those expectations.

ADDRESSING THE BEHAVIOR CONUNDRUM

Ultimately, we have a responsibility to all students to maximize their achievement and to close any gaps in their learning. Routinely, one of the major stumbling blocks that makes it difficult for educators to achieve this is the negative behaviors displayed by students and the lack of a universal approach to attending to those behaviors by adults.

Behavior has many components, and observing student behavior in context can provide great insights that will allow teachers to structure the best approach to help students close the gap and be on track for achieving the outcomes of the CCSS. Behavior can be an indicator, a communicator, functional, or a pattern revealer.

Behavior Is an Indicator

Experience tells me that the vast majority of our students want to behave, and will do so if they know how. It is puzzling that we take a different approach to academics than we do to behavior. Consider a student who enters a new grade. We don't expect that student to know all of the academics of the new grade, and we design fabulous and engaging lessons to impart the priority information we know they need to be successful. Yet that same student is expected to automatically know our behavior expectations, and if they do not comply with them, we structure consequences for their misbehavior. If a student is displaying negative behavior, it is a potential indicator of an underdeveloped skill, a lack of appropriate coping mechanisms, an adverse reaction to stress, or a lack of the basic prerequisite skill. The response needs to be the same as would occur when a student indicates an academic struggle—good lesson design, including a differentiated approach.

Behavior Is a Communicator

All behavior occurs for one of two reasons—to get something or to avoid something. No matter how erratic the behavior may seem, it is uniformly purposeful and often an unsophisticated attempt to solve a problem the student may be experiencing. Taking a step back and analyzing what students are trying to say through their behavior may yield more productive solutions than escalating the consequences.

Behavior Is Functional

As stated above, it's important to determine what the student is avoiding or getting through their behavior. Reminding students to raise their hands is a moot point if their desire is to get the teacher's attention. Being removed from a class in which the student struggles and being sent to a place where there are no demands will reinforce the negative behavior that resulted in that removal. Behavior becomes ingrained when the student gets something out of it. It is the response from others that results in a recurrence of inappropriate behavior. Teachers need to look for the reasons why the behavior is being displayed and then look for alternatives, so as to avoid reinforcing the unwanted behaviors.

Behavior Has a Pattern

With a little bit of analysis, we can often determine that behavior has a pattern. Perhaps the student struggles with an academic challenge on Monday mornings, or certain content areas (math), or at times of the day (just prior to lunch), or when a significant routine changes (a substitute teacher). Analyzing these can yield a better intervention than to routinely continue with the expectations and hope that the student will get up to speed. An "ABC analysis" that looks for the antecedents (A) to the behavior (B) will help to establish better consequences (C) that will shift the behavior to a more acceptable outcome. These antecedents are the strongest indicators, and awareness of them will help to create an intervention that precludes the behavior from occurring or escalating. A simple ABC analysis consists of the following:

1. Describe a student behavior (B) that concerns you.

2. Suggest some possible antecedents (A) or "triggers" for that behavior.

3. Suggest some possible consequences (C). These may be positive or negative things that reinforce the behavior. Ask: what does the student get or avoid by behaving that way?

Hierck, Coleman, and Weber (2011, pp. 60–61) provide an eight-step analysis that gives greater detail and clarity to this process.

The key to improving students' behavior usually begins with adults having their own behavior in check. Modeling expectations is a more powerful force for influence than delivering consequences. This is not to suggest that schools abandon any notion of consequences, but that consequences for bad behavior are used judiciously and only after good behavior lessons have been implemented. Behavior can be changed through an instructional approach. In designing this approach, schools should also support teachers in developing new approaches so they can interact with challenging students in a more productive and positive way.

In *Breaking the Behavior Code* (2012), Rappaport identifies five basic steps necessary to change inappropriate behavior to appropriate behavior for the long term.

1. **Manage antecedents.** This means minimizing or accommodating things in the environment that tend to set off an incident of inappropriate behavior. By understanding what antecedents are problematic for a student, such as being close to other students or reading aloud, the teacher can intervene effectively and create a classroom environment that is supportive and proactive.

2. **Reinforce desired behavior.** If a student can't tolerate academic demands without an outburst, the teacher may start by asking that student to do only 10 minutes of work, providing reinforcement, and over time building up the student's tolerance. As students demonstrate small attempts at self-regulation or the use of pro-social skills, the teacher should reinforce and reward them.

3. **Teach a replacement behavior.** Students need to be taught a replacement behavior—an appropriate behavior that serves the same function as the inappropriate behavior—to be used while building the skills

needed to behave appropriately without accommodations. For example, instead of banging fists on the desk when reading gets frustrating, a student could be taught to ask politely, "Can I have a break, please?"

4. **Address underdeveloped skills that are at the root of a student's inability to behave appropriately.** Teaching students underdeveloped skills eventually eliminates the need for the replacement behavior. For example, the fist-banging student may need to work on reading skills, perhaps with additional support.

5. **Respond to a student's inappropriate behavior in a way that deters it.** When prevention goes awry and incidents do occur, the teacher's response needs to reinforce the student's good behavior, and avoid accidentally reinforcing the undesired behavior.

When practiced and repeated, these steps define the expected outcomes and clarify the response that will occur when inappropriate behavior occurs. They lead to the establishment of a classroom environment that is conducive to maximum student learning and positive results.

Missed Opportunities

If we don't identify behavioral concerns, and if we don't have appropriate responses to intervene with, we risk continuing the approach that has been taken historically with students who struggle. It's an approach that has resulted in more than three million K–12 students who "lost instructional 'seat time' in 2009/2010 because they were suspended from school, often with no guarantee of adult supervision outside the school" (Losen and Gillespie, 2012). The more time students miss, the greater the academic gaps become and the less likely it becomes that the expectations of the CCSS—that students receive access to multiple means of learning and opportunities to demonstrate knowledge, but retain the rigor and high expectations—can be met. This downward spiral becomes a prime indicator of whether a child will drop out of school, and therefore have a greater likelihood of ultimately experiencing a lower socioeconomic status, poor health, and incarceration. One other significant point that Losen and Gillespie (2012) mention is that the chances of getting suspended are not the same for all students, as "African American children and children with disabilities are usually at a far greater risk than others."

MOVING FORWARD

All students who struggle, and especially those students identified under the Individuals with Disabilities Education Act (IDEA), must be given the opportunity to excel in school and be in a position to achieve success when they leave school and make the transition to college or a career. The Common Core provides a new opportunity, and an ambitious challenge, to ensure access to rigorous academic content for these students. The use of RTI strategies and the recognition that behavior and academics are inextricably linked gives educators access to the tools necessary to effect change in instructional design and practice. Effective implementation of these strategies can't help but improve access to mathematics and English language arts standards for all students, including those who struggle.

References

Buffum, A., Mattos, M., & Weber, C. (2009). *Pyramid response to intervention: RTI, professional learning communities, and how to respond when kids don't learn.* Bloomington, IN: Solution Tree.

Buffum, A., Mattos, M., & Weber, C. (2012). *Simplifying response to intervention: Four essential guiding principles.* Bloomington, IN: Solution Tree.

Hierck, T., Coleman, C., & Weber, C. (2011). *Pyramid of behavior interventions: Seven keys to a positive learning environment.* Bloomington, IN: Solution Tree.

Losen, D. J., & Gillespie, J. (2012). *Opportunities suspended: The disparate impact of disciplinary exclusion from school.* Los Angeles, CA: The Civil Rights Project at UCLA.

McNulty, R. J., & Gloeckler, L. C. (2011). *Fewer, clearer, higher common core state standards: Implications for students receiving special education services.* White Paper for the International Center for Leadership in Education.

National Governors Association Center for Best Practices & Council of Chief State School Officers (NGACBP & CCSSO). (2010). *Common core state standards.* Washington, DC: Authors.

Rappaport, N. (2012). *Breaking the behavior code.* Retrieved from http://www.psychologytoday.com/blog/we-are-only-human/ 201206/breaking-the-behavior-code

Ujifusa, A. (2013, June 27). Scores drop on Ky.'s common core-aligned tests. *Education Week.* Retrieved from http://www.edweek.org/ew/ articles/2012/11/02/11standards.h32.html

CHAPTER TWELVE

Effective Classroom Practices for High School Teachers:

Improving Engagement and Literacy

David Nagel

"We should focus on the greatest source of variance that can make the difference—the teacher."

JOHN HATTIE, 2003

FINANCIAL IMPLICATIONS OF MAINTAINING THE STATUS QUO IN AMERICAN HIGH SCHOOLS

At the time of this writing I have three boys, ages eight, three, and one. While each day brings new joys, and love I never thought possible, rarely does one day resemble the next. In my home life, I desire something that I cannot have right now: consistency. Any parent can relate to my dilemma. In my professional life, however,

I spend a great deal of time in one of the most consistent places or entities imaginable—American high schools. Our schools have been extremely consistent and reliable in producing similar results year after year. The National Center for Educational Statistics notes that from 1990 to 2009, four-year graduation rates deviated little from the 73.7 to 75.5 percent range. The number of dropouts alone is staggering, but even more alarming is the economic impact of those who do not graduate from high school. It is estimated that the nation spends more than $3.7 billion a year because too many students are not learning the basic skills needed to succeed in college or work while they are in high school (Alliance for Excellent Education, 2010).

EFFECTIVE INSTRUCTION
IS THE KEY

There are many actions high schools can take to reduce the number of students in danger of dropping out. What will have the greatest impact on achievement, often with the least amount of cost, are effective classroom instructional practices. John Hattie (2003) tells us that schools "need to ensure that the greatest influence (classroom teachers) is optimized to have powerful and sensationally positive effects on the learner." He goes on to state that teachers can and usually do have positive effects, but "they must have exceptional effects" (p. 4).

Think about anyone who is exceptional at something. Rarely are they good at *everything*, nor do they try to be. They concentrate on doing certain things really, really, well. A few strategies done well may have more impact than several or more that are ineffectively executed. In his book *Focus* (2011), Mike Schmoker tells us, "We cannot afford to over-complicate the elements of effective teaching" (p. 52). He goes on to remind us that we may be better served by focusing on a few practices that we know are effective and applying them to all students in a whole-class model.

REDUCING THE "ENGAGEMENT GAP"

A consistent challenge high schools face in their attempts to increase the graduation rate and decrease potential dropouts is a lack of student engagement. One of the main reasons students drop out of school is because they are bored and do not see the relevance or value of their work there. Dr. Ethan Yazzie-Mintz, the director of the High School Survey of Student Engagement, calls this the "engagement gap" (2009, p. 16). Effective instructional models in high schools hinge on the teacher's ability to engage students and connect their learning in meaningful and relevant ways.

The adoption and implementation of the Common Core standards has created new challenges for high school teachers because of increased demands in rigor. But the CCSS also provide a new opportunity to leverage engagement with students. The standards, which place a greater emphasis on reading and writing at more rigorous levels, were designed to promote literacy as a shared responsibility across disciplines. There are specific practices and strategies that high school teachers can implement immediately in their classrooms that will have a positive impact on achievement through increasing engagement and strengthening literacy.

STRATEGY 1:
LEVERAGING STUDENT LEARNING

The principle of leverage in education is related to the application of a standard to multiple academic disciplines. "Student proficiency in nonfiction writing is directly related to student success in reading, mathematics, social studies, and science" (Reeves, 2002). Assisting students in making connections from one course to another should be a priority for all high school teachers, if for no other reason, to limit the isolation of learning. In a typical high school English classroom, most teachers would expect the students to give their all for 57 minutes to the English content. When the bell rings, the students hit the hallway, use the restroom, find their friends, and perhaps send a few text messages before going to biology, where that teacher now expects the students to give their all for 57 minutes to biology content. This is most often done without any thought or consideration of what the student just learned in English. The National Association of Secondary School Principals' *Breaking Ranks II* (2004) framework recommends that high schools "integrate the school's curriculum to the extent possible and emphasize depth over breadth of coverage." The more we can make this happen, the more we can engage students and help them connect their learning from one classroom to another.

Authentic Performance Tasks

Authentic performance tasks with real-world applications allow students to apply deeper levels of learning while providing relevance to increase engagement. The Common Core standards are rich in their rigor, but they are also rich in their intent that teachers focus instruction and assessment around tasks and processes that assist students in discovering—not just remembering—answers. Tasks that provide students with an opportunity to synthesize information, connect learning across disciplines, and address literacy standards are a way for high school teachers to get a "bigger bang for their buck."

Teachers do this by designing engaging tasks focused on their own content areas while utilizing the Common Core literacy standards as a link to help students connect the learning with other subjects in meaningful ways. The Leadership and Learning Center's model for performance assessment guides teachers through a process of designing engaging tasks that are targeted to "unwrapped" Priority Standards. Literacy connections through Common Core standards provide students and teachers with a common link when creating tasks that can be designed to increase leverage of standards and content across disciplines.

Purposeful, Productive, and Collaborative Group Work

The key to making group work engaging to students as well as useful to teachers is that it be purposeful, productive, and collaborative.

Purposeful: The group is focused on a specific task linked to a specific standard.

Productive: Groups will be responsible for turning out a final result or product.

Collaborative: Students will *need* to work together on solutions and products.

High School Survey of Student Engagement data show that most students (60 percent) rated group projects as "exciting and engaging"; only a small proportion of students (16 percent) rated group projects low (Yazzie-Mintz, 2009). In addition to increased engagement, students learn more quickly in groups than by themselves (Johnson and Johnson, 2004). Effective collaborative group work provides a deeper level of engagement for students by adding accountability and responsibility toward each other. This aligns directly with a key intention of the Common Core speaking and listening standards: "students will collaborate to answer questions, build understanding, and solve problems."

Embedded Formative Assessment and Differentiation

Collaborative learning facilitates increased formative assessment and differentiated instruction. Student groups often progress at different levels through tasks toward the creation of a final product. This allows teachers to provide on-the-spot feedback to different groups at different stages in the learning progression.

Differentiation can also happen more naturally and on the fly as student groups are moving toward developing their final product. As students are progressing on the task or problem given, teachers can scaffold specific instruction to provide some teams with short-term learning targets while offering teams that are ready additional challenges and opportunities for growth. An example that aligns with the Common Core recommendations of how to provide enrichment for groups that need additional challenges is to have them synthesize information from additional sources and use texts that are more complex.

Increasing Metacognition

Collaborative work naturally increases metacognition, or "thinking about thinking." When students are working and processing in a group setting, they learn how to use particular strategies for problem solving (Metcalfe and Shimamura, 1994). The first Common Core mathematical practice standard states that students should "make sense of problems and persevere in solving them." Effective collaborative learning models provide students with a greater opportunity to share personal new learning discoveries with peers about how they are figuring out how to figure things out.

Here are some directions that teachers can have students respond to, to increase metacognition at the end of a peer collaboration activity:

- Give an example of something the others in the group have learned from you.
- Give a suggestion of a change the group could make that would improve everyone's learning.

Limiting Ineffectiveness of Group Work

Collaborative learning is one of the most abused and at times ineffectively used strategies. Larson and Keiper (2013) note that parents and students often have a negative view of group work from previous experiences with it. This stems from prior group projects where only one or two students had to do all of the work. A recommendation Frey, Fisher, and Allen (2009) make to increase the "productivity" of the group is to create more positive interdependence. This simply means that not every member carries the same load, but the participation of every member is essential to successful completion of the task.

Specific actions teachers can take to increase the effectiveness of collaborative group work include:

- Requiring group members to work together in order to earn any individual recognition (Slavin, 1989/1990)

- Intentionally placing students in groups rather than allowing them to self-select (Johnson and Johnson, 2004)

- Randomly placing students in heterogeneous groups at least one time per week (Marzano, Pickering, and Pollock, 2001)

- Having a system or structure to ensure that groups have proper support from peers or teachers

- Having teachers design collaborative learning activities with peer evaluations, and grade individual contributions to reduce students relying on their group members to "carry the load"

Example of Leveraging Authentic Performance Tasks and Collaborative Group Work

Four high school teachers collaborated to create the lessons in Figure 12.1. They all applied primary and supporting Common Core literacy standards for writing and speaking and listening to a set of collaborative group tasks in their tenth-grade classrooms. Tasks were created to assist students in connecting content from one class to another (earth science paired with algebra and English language arts paired with U.S. history).

Primary Standards:

W.9–10.1 Write arguments to support claims in an analysis of substantive topics or texts using valid reasoning and relevant and sufficient evidence.

WHST.9–10.1 Write arguments focused on discipline-specific content to support claims in an analysis of substantive topics or texts using valid reasoning and relevant and sufficient evidence.

SL.9–10.1 Initiate and participate effectively in a range of collaborative discussions.

Supporting Standards:

SL.9–10.1d Respond thoughtfully to diverse perspectives. Summarize points of agreement and disagreement.

W.9-10.6 Use technology, including the Internet, to produce, publish, and update individual or shared writing products, taking advantage of technology's capacity to link to other information and to display information flexibly and dynamically.

FIGURE 12.1	Leveraging Lessons		

Course/ Subject	Common Core Skills	Key Concept	Lesson Idea/Product Example with Connection to Other Discipline
Science (earth science)	• Write arguments • Collaborate with others • Produce and distribute writing • Summarize points of agreement and disagreement	Claims (support)	Students collect data and information on the risks of possible earthquakes in "lower-risk" areas and what probability exists for a quake to occur and damage existing structures. Students collaborate in pairs or triads to create and design a one-page brochure that summarizes and supports their claim of whether or not it is cost effective to build additional supports in new buildings in this area. (Connects with math)
Math (algebra 2)	• Write arguments • Collaborate with others • Use technology to publish writing • Summarize points of agreement and disagreement	Claims (support)	In groups of 3–4, based on mathematical formulas, students will defend or argue in writing for or against money being spent to structurally support existing buildings in "low risk" areas for earthquake damage. This would be in newspaper editorial format for possible print or Internet-based posting. (Connects with science)

FIGURE 12.1	**Leveraging Lessons** (continued)

Course/ Subject	Common Core Skills	Key Concept	Lesson Idea/Product Example with Connection to Other Discipline
English language arts	• Write arguments • Collaborate with others • Produce and distribute writing • Summarize points of agreement and disagreement	Claims (support)	After reading one of the four sections of the book *Hiroshima*, as well as several pieces that highlight accurate description of U.S. intelligence in 1945, students work in pairs or triads to argue their support for or against Truman's decision to drop the atomic bomb. Students write a terse newspaper article supporting or condemning the decision with facts and testimony from the accounts from *Hiroshima*, as well as evidence from other sources. (Connects with social studies)
Social studies (U.S. history)	• Write arguments • Collaborate with others • Use technology to publish writing • Summarize points of agreement and disagreement	Claims (support)	Students study all of the possible scenarios/options Truman had *at the time of the bombing* to make his decision. Students collect information from multiple fact-based nonfiction texts and other sources. Working in pairs or triads, students then create a Web site or Facebook page with specific evidence that defends or argues for or against whether Truman's decision was that of absolute certainty in dropping the bomb. Students must comment on 10 or more peer pages as to their level of agreement or disagreement with valid reasoning and argument (30 words or less). (Connects with language arts)

Busy high school teachers rarely have time to be fully aware of the content, curriculum, and pacing guides of teachers in other disciplines. To overcome this, at the start of the school year teachers at Central High School in Tulsa, Oklahoma, listed all of their main content topics by quarter and by individual course on chart paper. Teachers did a gallery walk to see where there were specific connections from their courses to others. For example, algebra teachers determined that they could focus on probability at the same time the biology teachers were doing so in genetics. Each time teachers intentionally try to help more students make connections, they engage more students.

STRATEGY 2:
CONCEPT ATTAINMENT

"To put the matter bluntly, a high school graduate who is a poor reader is a postsecondary student who must struggle mightily to succeed" (National Governors Association Center for Best Practices and Council of Chief State School Officers, 2010). The Common Core standards call for students to read and comprehend at increased levels of text complexity. This is one of the major shifts needed instructionally for all students to be successful with the more rigorous demands of the Common Core. High school students must be able to comprehend at higher levels of cognitive functioning or they will not have the capacity to be successful with texts they will encounter in future work or college pathways (NGACBP and CCSSO, 2010; ACT, 2005, p. 16). Using more complex texts, students will need to be able to distinguish relevant information from extraneous as well as be able to identify key attributes of critical concepts.

Based primarily on Jerome Bruner's 1977 research, Larson and Keiper refer to concept attainment as "concept formation," where students "form robust understandings of significant concepts in content areas" (2013, p. 175). They describe students working through a process to understand a concept, and assert that simply telling students about the concept is insufficient. Concepts selected should be those that are difficult for students and are important for future lessons.

Selecting Concepts

The teacher first decides which concept(s) are important to the lesson or unit, and determines the important attributes of each concept. Larson and Keiper describe two types of concepts: established concepts (with easily defined attributes: rock cycle, government, theme), and dynamic concepts (with more disagreement: reliability, freedom, love) (2013, p. 191). If the teacher cannot identify at least three to five critical attributes of a concept, then this strategy is not recommended (p. 179).

After some instruction that will involve reading nonfiction texts about the concept(s), the teacher will ask the students to assist in coming up with some of the attributes of the concept being introduced. This should be done on a chart, whiteboard, or other place viewable by all students. Students are given time to process and converse with peers about what the attributes have and do not have in common. Students then try to create some common themes from the lists. Teachers then provide students with a starting list of *some* concrete examples and nonexamples of the concept. Students are then given time to add concrete examples while they are processing the information from reading the text as well as the teacher's examples. The teacher will pose questions as students are generating more examples, such as: How are they similar? How are they different?

Concept Attainment in Action

In a tenth-grade biology class, a teacher guides her students through analyzing the relationships between two important concepts for a unit on diseases and pathogens: bacteria vs. viruses. After students read a section from the textbook and a science journal related to the two concepts, the teacher guides students through key attributes and nonattributes of bacteria. She lists these one at a time on her SMART Board (the results are shown in Figure 12.2). After providing the students with some processing time, students create on their own some examples and nonexamples, demonstrating their new understanding of the concept of bacteria. (The nonexamples are related to viruses.)

FIGURE 12.2	Concept Attainment Activity Example		
Attributes	**Nonattributes**	**Examples**	**Nonexamples**
DNA	Has a nucleus	Botulism	Polio
Heterotrophs	Multi-cellular	Yogurt	Influenza
Used in some foods	Requires Oxygen	Lactobacillus	AIDS
Autotrophs	Larger Cell Size	Strep Throat	Warts
Can cause disease	Complex Cells	Meningitis	Cold Sores
Killed by antibiotic	Many organelles		
Can reproduce on own	More time to divide		

The Common Core literacy standard being addressed is **RST.9–10.5**: Analyze the structure of the relationships among concepts in a text, including relationships among key terms (e.g., force, friction, reaction force, energy).

STRATEGY 3: INCREASE WRITING

U.S. corporations spend an estimated $3.1 billion annually to remediate their employees' writing skills, and state governments spend an estimated $221 million annually for the same purpose (National Commission on Writing, 2005).

In 2006, a sizable number of high school students reported in a survey that they never or hardly ever wrote a paper three pages or longer in their language arts class during their high school careers. Likewise, 60 percent of students did not write a paragraph or more in social studies and 80 percent did not write a paragraph or more in science more than once a week (Applebee and Langer, 2006).

Common Core anchor standard 10 for writing states that students must "write routinely over extended time frames (time for research, reflection, and revision) and shorter time frames (a single sitting or a day or two) for a range of tasks, purposes, and audiences." In science, history, and technical subjects the standard differs slightly by adding the words "discipline specific." Even in these non-language-arts classes, writing on demand should be a consistent instructional practice.

Providing More Opportunities to Hook Students

Many high school teachers express frustration when attempting to get reluctant students to write, especially when prompted to do so on demand. An effective strategy to persuade more students to at least *begin* the process of writing and not just shut down and quit before they start is creating multifaceted writing prompts with multiple questions for students to address. The rationale is that if students have little interest in the single writing prompt provided, they may shut down and write little or nothing because of a lack of engagement. In *Rain, Steam, and Speed*, Fleming and Pike-Baky describe how having multiple prompts can often "jump start" the student writing process (2005, p. 5).

Designing Effective Writing Prompts

When teachers are creating writing prompts for their students for an on-demand writing assignment, the key is that they create multiple prompts and multiple questions in an attempt to offer as many chances to "hook" the students as they can. Teachers design both primary and supplementary prompts. These are related to the specific content and topics currently being taught and covered in the class. Primary prompts will address key concepts and topics covered during the recent instruction. Students will be required to select at least one of these primary prompts or statements to address. This ensures that students are responding to important concepts and essential questions related to the class. Students are also provided with supplementary prompts to be used as links or mechanisms to address in more detail the primary writing prompt.

Addressing Time and Feedback

As students are given an on-demand writing opportunity to address specific prompts and questions directly tied to the current content of the class, they should be given a defined period to write and respond. While quality is always of primary importance, the feedback initially should focus on the quantity of writing that specifically addresses the content-based prompt(s), and less on grammar and other language mechanics. A simple rubric should be provided to ensure the writing is targeted to the content-based prompt. For example, if students do successfully address the prompts provided content-wise, their grade or points or marks should initially come from quantity: 1.5 pages = A; 1 page = B; and 0.5 pages = C, with no exceptions. The initial goal of the strategy is to get students to write *more* and *on demand.* Students are often limited in how much they write to ensure they focus their ideas.

Figure 12.3 shows example writing prompts, and Figure 12.4 shows a sample rubric.

| FIGURE 12.3 | Writing Prompts | |

Course	Description	Examples
Social Studies (American History)	After studying the concept of "freedom," related to the unit on the U.S. Constitution, students will read a specific article that addresses either gun control or the Roe v. Wade decision. Students will respond to one of the primary prompts as well as respond to one or more of the supplementary prompts for an on-demand writing task.	**Primary Prompts:** • What is freedom? • How do you know you have that as an American? • What are some freedoms that you feel are infringed upon here at school? **Supplementary Prompts:** • What aspects of gun control do you feel infringe on the Second Amendment? • If you were a gun holder, how would you feel about losing that right? • How does Roe v. Wade impact the freedoms of women? • How does it impact the freedoms of the unborn?
Biology	As a "pop assessment" during the unit on cell function, students are given 25 minutes to address one of the primary and supplementary prompts listed.	**Primary Prompts:** • What are cells? • How do different types of cells interact with each other in the human body? **Supplementary Prompts:** • How does a cell resemble a factory or other system with interacting parts and mechanisms? • If you could be a cell in the human body, what type would you be and why?
Band or Choir	After a recent competition/performance, students are asked to respond in writing to the following prompts. (Students are not directed to address any one specific prompt.)	**Primary Prompts:** • How do you feel your group performed Saturday? • What do you feel your group did well? • Why do you think that was the case? • What will you take away to work on next time? • What do you feel your group could have done better? • How could you individually and as a group work on that this week during class, practice, and rehearsal?

FIGURE 12.4	Writing Rubric	

Grade	Quantity	Quality
A	1.5 pages, but not more than 2 pages	• Specifically addresses one of the primary prompts and at least two of the supplementary prompts. • Contains at least three key points with correct and specific content examples cited in the writing supporting both the primary and supplementary prompts. • Has fewer than 3-4 major grammatical errors that do not limit readability.
B	1.0 page	• Specifically addresses one of the primary prompts and at least one of the supplementary prompts. • Contains at least two key points with correct and specific content examples cited in the writing. • Has fewer than 3–4 major grammatical errors that do not limit readability.
C	At least 0.5 page	• Specifically addresses one of the primary prompts and at least one of the supplementary prompts. • Contains at least one key point with correct and specific content examples cited in the writing. • Has fewer than 3–4 major grammatical errors that do not limit readability.

Applicability to Electives

Teaching literacy is a responsibility shared by every teacher in high schools. This is a scary proposition for some teachers, who rightfully feel they do not have adequate training and professional development to teach, coach, and assess writing. Elective-area teachers express this concern the most.

Ben Davis High School, in Indianapolis, has a marching band that is one of the most successful in the midwest, as well as the nation. They have participated in the Tournament of Roses Parade more than any school in the nation outside the state of California. For several years, the band directors have been using multifaceted writing prompts. In doing so, they have learned a great deal about how their students are processing and applying the music-based instruction they are providing.

Several years ago, after administering a writing prompt assignment after a band competition, the directors pulled seven to eight samples from two specific groups of student musicians: the percussion and low brass. Neither the students nor the directors were focusing on grammar and mechanics but just on the ideas and content that the students were sharing through the activity. The directors were very excited about what they learned about the connections and take-aways the students were making. The directors found a common error that specific groups of students were making related to transitions and beat. Associate Band Director Shawn McNabb said, "By reading basically the same take-away from three to four students, it was apparent in their collective processing the error they were all making. We were able to address it immediately and improve drastically in one week's time. I am confident without having them process through writing, we would not have identified the common misconception."

FOSTERING SUCCESS

Engagement and literacy have proved to be critical factors leading to student success or failure in high school. Knowing this, classroom strategies and practices must focus on both consistently. Each of the three strategies above can be easily adapted into any high school classroom. When implementing these strategies—or any strategy or practice—high school teachers must first concentrate on ways to engage students, with an intentional focus on improving students' skills in reading and writing. The Common Core standards for literacy can be the catalyst for any discipline. This may be the greatest way to follow John Hattie's (2003) recommendation that we must ensure that "excellent teachers have exceptional effects with students."

References

ACT. (2005). Crisis at the core: Preparing all students for college and work. *Activity 43*(1). Retrieved from www.act.org/activity/winter2005/crisis.html

Alliance for Excellent Education. (2010, September). High school dropouts in America (Fact sheet). Retrieved from www.all4ed.org/files/HighSchoolDropouts.pdf

Applebee, A., & Langer, J. (2006). *The state of writing instruction in America's schools: What existing data tell us.* Albany, NY: Center on English Learning and Achievement.

Fleming, G., & Pike-Baky, M. (2005). *Rain, steam, and speed: Building fluency in adolescent writers.* San Francisco, CA: Jossey-Bass.

Frey, N., Fisher, D., & Allen, A. (2009). Productive group work in middle and high school classrooms. In S. R. Parris, D. Fisher, & K. Headley (Eds.), *Adolescent literacy, field tested* (pp. 70–81). Newark, DE: International Reading Association.

Hattie, J. (2003, October). *Teachers make a difference: What is the research evidence?* University of Auckland. Australian Council for Educational Research.

Johnson, D. W., & Johnson, R. T. (2004). *Assessing students in groups: Promoting group responsibility and individual accountability.* Thousand Oaks, CA: Corwin.

Larson, B., & Keiper, T. (2013). *Instructional strategies for middle and high school* (2nd ed.). New York, NY: Routledge.

Marzano, R. J., Pickering, D. J., & Pollock, J. E. (2001). *Classroom instruction that works: Research-based strategies for increasing student achievement.* Alexandria, VA: ASCD.

Metcalfe, J., & Shimamura, A. P. (1994). *Metacognition: Knowing about knowing.* Cambridge, MA: MIT Press.

National Association of Secondary School Principals. (2004). *Breaking ranks II: Strategies for leading high school reform* (executive summary). Retrieved from http://www.nassp.org/Content/ 158/BRII_exec_summary.pdf

National Center for Education Statistics. (Multiple dates). NCES common core of data state dropout and completion data file, school year 2007–08; 2008–09, version 1a; and State nonfiscal survey of public elementary/secondary education, 1990–91, version 1b; 1995–96, version 1b; 2000–01, version 1b; 2005–06, version 1b, and 2006–07, version 1b. Retrieved from http://nces.ed.gov/ ccd/drpcompstatelvl.asp

National Commission on Writing for America's Families, Schools, and Colleges. (2005). *Writing: A powerful message from state government.* New York, NY: The College Board.

National Governors Association Center for Best Practices & Council of Chief State School Officers (NGACBP & CCSSO). (2010). *Common core state standards.* Washington, DC: Authors.

Reeves, D. B. (2002). *Making standards work: How to implement standards-based assessments in the classroom, school, and district* (3rd ed.). Englewood, CO: Advanced Learning Press.

Schmoker, M. (2011). *Focus: Elevating the essentials to radically improve student learning.* Alexandria, VA: ASCD.

Slavin, R. (1989/1990). Guest editorial: Here to stay—or gone tomorrow? *Educational Leadership, 47*(4), 3.

Yazzie-Mintz, E. (2009). *Engaging the voices of students: A report on the 2007 & 2008 high school survey of student engagement.* Retrieved from http://www.indiana.edu/~ceep/hssse/images/HSSSE _2009_Report.pdf

CHAPTER THIRTEEN

Success in the Beginning:

Supporting New Teachers

Lynn Howard

"Today I say thank you for the experience of being a part of the new teacher program! I believe that I am an effective, classroom management, cooperative learning activity, student-teacher relationship building, qualified EDUCATOR! The process made ALL the difference."

NEW TEACHER

Imagine a classroom full of children. They have a variety of learning styles, levels of ability, and prior knowledge, and they come from all kinds of families. Some are gifted, some are emotionally challenged, some are poor readers, and some are hyperactive. Many love school and love to learn, while others are content to just work in the family business. The teacher loves her job, but teaching to the standards is difficult in a mixed-ability class where special strategies to help struggling students are required. Her class is technologically lacking, and supplies often run out before the end of the year. Climate control is near to impossible, as it is either freezing cold or stifling hot. The teacher is attending classes herself to further her knowledge and keep it up-to-date. This is the situation that Laura Ingalls Wilder faced in 1882 as she began her teaching career at the age of 15. Although many things have changed in education, there are startling similarities as well. It has never been easy to be a new teacher faced with a classroom full of children for the first time.

WOULD YOU WANT TO BE A NEW TEACHER TODAY?

Veteran educators give mixed answers to this question. When a group of experienced teachers was asked to brainstorm all the roles, responsibilities, and "things" that were required in teaching, the teachers generated a list of more than 100 items. It included everything from how to get students to line up, to lesson planning, to parent conferences and substitutes. One of the most daunting tasks is that of understanding and implementing the new standards, whether the Common Core State Standards (CCSS) for math and English language arts or the Next Generation Science Standards (NGSS). All teachers will need guidance and support as they design their classroom atmosphere and plan units of study with specific lessons focused around the new standards. The challenge for new teachers (and veteran teachers) is to learn the format of the standards and related content, the best instructional strategies, and the assessment implications. Take a minute to think about all of the things that must be learned and how prepared you were on your first day. Now think about what you are doing to prepare new educators in your school for these challenges.

Catherine did not start out as an exemplary teacher. She entered the education profession in a lateral entry position with no formal training or coursework. Her degree was in French and religion; her assignment was reading and two classes each of introductory French and Spanish. Catherine called me for help. Working with a first-year teacher was difficult, and demanded extreme effort and patience from both of us. Catherine was determined to be the best teacher in the world, but it became obvious from her questions that she had no clue what to expect from the first day. We spent a year together, planning and designing "what works for Catherine" and the best instructional practices for her students. Weekends were dedicated to lesson plans, discipline issues, and conflicts with administration and parents. Our work together necessitated a careful balance between her enthusiastic naïveté and my long years of experience. I saw the passion and commitment that she brought to her job and we constantly laughed at my favorite phrase: *"Do not quit."* This experience awoke in me a special passion for new teachers. I will always remember one of Catherine's comments to me during that first year: "I want to be just like you. You were the best seventh-grade teacher anyone could ever have." What could you say to that?

This experience made it very clear that what my district was doing to support new teachers was not enough. Catherine had been to two days of "Rookie Camp" prior to the start of school, but was totally unprepared for the first day.

Whether you are looking for strategies and ideas to begin a new teacher support process or ideas to support an existing program, it is important to realize that teacher retention is a process, not a program, and should be a year-long commitment that includes your entire school community. The suggestions and ideas presented in the following pages are integral strategies from *Ready for Anything: Supporting New Teachers for Success* (Howard, 2006), and are appropriate for K–12 educators in all school settings.

THE GOAL

The goal of a new teacher support process is to have the teacher want to return to the same school next year. The ownership of teacher retention should be site-based, and should provide a continuous, seamless flow of professional development targeted at skill and knowledge development for all teachers. New teacher support should:

- Provide new teachers with sustained professional development that is relevant, grade-level specific, and modeled after Learning Forward's *Standards for Professional Learning* (2012).

- Provide support in implementing the standards used by their district (e.g., CCSS math or ELA, or the Next Generation Science Standards).

- Supply teachers with research-based strategies, including strategies for organization, classroom management, instruction, and assessment.

- Give administrators a collaborative support model for teacher retention.

- Improve the level of teacher satisfaction regarding working conditions and school climate.

- Raise student achievement though teacher instruction and student-centered learning.

• Build capacity through a new teacher mentor process where new teachers can observe a master teacher implementing instructional strategies aligned with the standards.

RECRUIT OR RETAIN?

Is it better to recruit or retain? It is imperative that schools, with principals as their instructional leaders, address the problem of teacher retention. More than 40 percent of the current teaching force will be leaving within the next two years, creating a huge demand for new teachers. National teacher turnover rates, along with individual school district results (both urban and rural), have guided the development and implementation of effective induction processes. Teacher turnover data from Ingersoll (2003 and 2001), Darling-Hammond (1997), and state education departments all indicate that there is growing concern about recruiting and retaining qualified educators. Recent data indicate that 17 percent of teachers leave after one year, 30 percent of teachers leave after two years, 40 percent leave after three years, and 50 percent leave after five years (Ingersoll, 2003).

DEFINING A NEW TEACHER

Mr. Johnson was a new teacher in the largest middle school in the state. He had just left a career with a large technology company and wanted to make a difference with children, so he chose teaching as his next career. Teaching science to eighth graders was a daunting challenge, and nothing had prepared him for the multiple facets of managing a classroom, understanding new content standards, and relating to the school community and his colleagues. We often think of "new" teachers as those leaving college and beginning a career in education, but with the downsizing of major companies, many people are entering the teaching profession as a second or third career choice. The term "new teacher" can refer to multiple types of people these days.

For the purposes of new teacher support, a new teacher or beginning teacher can be one with no prior background or experience; with certification and college coursework, but no experience; or with experience, but recently hired from a different district or school system. You should make an individual determination as to which teachers would benefit most from new teacher support at your school.

DESIGNING SUPPORT

New teachers need *everything*! I met with a group of 117 new teachers recently before the first day of school. A lot of information was shared during the two days we spent together. At the end of the second day, I asked them if they had any questions, and the room was dead silent. Not a single person had a question. I met with them again after their first day with students, and they could not stop raising their hands; they had hundreds of logistical questions.

Ready for Anything: Supporting New Teachers for Success (Howard, 2006) recommends that new teacher support be planned well in advance of the first day of implementation. The teachers' needs should be identified by a team so that a year-long calendar of events can be planned and organized. You should determine, based on your school, what skills and knowledge your new teachers will need to be successful with the students in your building. The people who will implement the process are critical, and must be carefully selected to facilitate the program, with the principal having responsibility for the success of the staff.

Surveys of new teachers find that there are three overall concerns about entering the teaching profession. The feeling of being isolated and not knowing that they are having the same problems as other teachers is very prevalent in new teachers. Many of them don't know how to ask for help, and will continue to struggle unless someone is monitoring and checking on them. A lack of support from the principal and a lack of personal interaction on a regular basis contribute to that isolation. Principals that visit new teacher classrooms and provide a quick note of encouragement build capacity at a quicker pace than those who are not visible. The number one concern among new teachers is classroom management. One of my new teachers says that working with middle school students is like "herding mosquitoes." Most of your new teachers are not "people managers"; some have had no previous classroom experience, and they become frustrated very quickly when students do not follow the rules and their instructions.

SUGGESTIONS FOR A
NEW TEACHER SUPPORT PROCESS

One suggestion for supporting your new teachers is to design monthly seminars that will form the framework for what effective teachers should know and be able to do. These can be either on-site at your school or in combination with other schools. The seminars should all have the same format, including a goal, focus, agenda, strategies, and reflective time. You will want to model and practice classroom activities that new teachers can immediately take back and use with their students. The key is to include strategies that address classroom management and student engagement in every seminar. It is very easy to overwhelm a new teacher with too many things, and pacing out the strategies, over time, will give them a chance to practice and to develop a strong toolbox of activities to use in their classrooms.

Although not at all inclusive, the following list contains seminar topics and activities that have proved to be productive as new teachers begin a school year:

Getting Ready for the First Week of School

- *Do not* read the teacher handbook out loud to new teachers. Point out only the components that will help during the first week of school, or better yet, design interactive tasks that will help them learn those components; the rest will come.

- Take teachers on a scavenger hunt of the school.

- Give them a "new teacher" box of goodies and supplies.

- Design a "special request" form that they can use to communicate needs to you.

- Provide a general list of supplies that they should have for their classroom.

- Model and provide several opening-of-school activities that they could use with their students during the first week (e.g., classroom scavenger hunt, people bingo).

- Give new teachers a copy of their grade-level standards and provide time to explore and get an understanding of their own classroom implications.

Classroom Atmosphere

- Talk about the physical characteristics of setting up their classroom.

- Spend a lot of time talking about building relationships with students.

- Model and practice positive reinforcement strategies for celebrating success.

- Provide examples of classroom displays that highlight student work samples.

- Take teachers on a "classroom crawl" of each other's classrooms to see what ideas they can take back to their own classrooms.

- Talk about the implications of the science and engineering practices from the NGSS, the Common Core's mathematical practice standards, and the Common Core's ELA student capacities, and the impact they have on building effective classroom relationships.

Classroom Management

- Teach about procedures and give a generic list of classroom procedures that students should follow.

- Talk about the use of positive behavior strategies such as phone calls and notes for students.

- Follow up with each new teacher's management plan and spend time supporting the implementation of their classroom procedures.
- Differentiate classroom management strategies by content areas (e.g., science lab procedures, art instruction, music practices).

Using Standards to Plan Units and Lessons

- Provide time to understand the standards (e.g., CCSS math and ELA, and NGSS).
- Teach teachers to "unwrap" their grade-level standards (Ainsworth, 2003).
- Provide exemplars of lesson plans and talk about the pieces that make good instructional presentations.
- Monitor and provide feedback on their lesson plans.

Engaging and Motivating Instructional Strategies

- Select instructional strategies that apply to all grade levels and content as related to the CCSS and the NGSS.
- Model and practice teacher-directed and student-centered strategies to use with students. Integrate these into your staff meetings so that all can benefit.
- Show all teachers how to integrate reading, writing, and vocabulary into their grade-level content areas.
- Differentiate literacy strategies and model implementation based on content areas.
- Provide time for your new teachers to meet with and observe their mentors and other master teachers.

Observations, Evaluations, and Feedback

- Provide descriptions, explanations, and specific examples of what is expected during classroom walkthroughs and formal observations.

- Use the "evidence of effective teaching matrix" in *Ready for Anything: Supporting New Teachers for Success* (Howard, 2006) as a guide to classroom evidence and questions for discussion and reflection.

- Provide examples of classroom practices that align with the CCSS and NGSS that would be included on a walkthrough form.

Stress Management

- Take time to play and have a bit of fun (small toys and bottles of bubble solution can provide a lot of entertainment).

- Have new teachers discuss their stress points and offer solutions for reducing in- and out-of-class tensions.

- Provide time for new teachers to observe and collaborate with other new teachers so that they don't feel so isolated.

The Rules of State and Local Testing

- Talk about your testing code of ethics.

- Provide test-taking strategies that teachers can use with their students.

- Tell everyone what to expect the week before and the day of testing.

- Provide time to explore and examples of the next generation assessment systems (e.g., Partnership for Assessment of Readiness for College and Careers, Smarter Balanced Assessment Consortium, Achieve).

Surviving the Last Weeks of School

- Give teachers a "teacher checkout form" prior to the last day of school and talk about the who, what, when, and where of what needs to happen prior to leaving.

- Celebrate the end of the year with certificates, recognitions, and a fun event.

THE ROLE OF THE PRINCIPAL

It is the school principal who has the knowledge, resources, and responsibility to take ownership as the primary influence on the success of a new teacher. As a principal and administrator, take a moment to reflect back on your first day of classroom teaching. Do you remember what type of support you had? Or do you remember just being assigned a room and given a key? Many teachers have the opportunity to have a supportive mentor or to take college courses that guide and direct them along the path of education success. Teacher exit surveys indicate that one of the most common reasons teachers leave is lack of support from the administration, specifically the principal. Many teachers remark that although tangible items are very useful in the classroom, it is personal interaction and communication with the principal that make the ultimate difference in their decision to return to or leave a particular school. When the principal makes a concerted effort to create conditions that support and nurture new staff, teacher retention is more likely.

"School leaders should not only run efficient, safe and caring learning environments—they should also be leaders of teaching and learning" (Robinson, 2006, p. 62). Robinson's research indicates that leading teacher learning and development has an effect size of 0.84, which is significant for student achievement. The more leaders focus their relationships, their work, and their learning on the core business of teaching and learning, the greater their influence on student outcomes.

Direct instructional leadership is focused on the quality of teacher practice, including the quality of the curriculum, teaching, assessment, and teacher inquiry and learning. Indirect instructional leadership creates the conditions for good teaching and teacher learning by ensuring that school policies, routines, resourcing, and other management decisions support and require high-quality learning, teaching, and teacher learning (Kleine-Kracht, 1993). Both types of leadership are necessary for effective schools, but the principal must be the instructional leader as school reform and improvement occurs throughout the country.

Guiding Questions and Ideas for Principals

Before beginning or supplementing a new teacher support process, take time to review the following guiding questions and reflect on your current practices. What are you doing well? Where can you make improvements? How have you implemented your own personal action growth plan?

- Do you spend time with your new teachers, visiting their classrooms and looking at how effective they are at organization, management, and instruction?

- What type of feedback do you provide each time you visit a classroom?
- Have you personally checked to make sure your teachers have the necessary materials and resources?
- Do you allow time at staff meetings to share exemplary teaching methods and strategies?
- Have you set aside informal time just to meet with new teachers?
- Did you assign a master teacher within the same grade level or content area as a mentor for each new teacher? Do you provide uninterrupted time for them to meet?
- How do you value the strengths of each staff member and use their talents for the betterment of the school?
- Have you provided a time for new teachers to network and observe master teachers, both at your school and at others?
- Have you investigated additional ways to support your teachers? What are your colleagues doing in their schools?
- Did you try to provide a classroom and no extra duties for your new teachers?
- Do you attend professional development with your teachers and model best practices at staff meetings?

New teachers have specified five areas in which the principal can positively influence their success and desire to work toward a productive career in education:

1. Have an open-door policy and make time to share and discuss issues, concerns, and successes without fear of intimidation or retaliation.

2. Supply the resources and give the support needed to integrate and align teachers with the vision and mission of the school.

3. Establish a time for teachers to meet with other teachers to plan instruction aligned to the standards (e.g., CCSS and NGSS) and to discuss assessment practices.

4. Create an environment that encourages celebration, safety, and professionalism.

5. Encourage and provide quality professional development in needed skills and knowledge areas, particularly classroom management and instructional strategies.

STRATEGIES FOR PRINCIPALS

There are many strategies that administrators can implement that help support their new teachers. Select several of the following activities from *Ready for Anything: Supporting New Teachers for Success* (Howard, 2006) to implement during the year. Whatever you choose, remember that the key to success is consistency, so maintain your plan.

Welcome to the Teaching Profession: Plan several opening-of-school activities, such as a school scavenger hunt, a person bingo, or a basket full of supplies for new teachers.

Just Checking on You Today: Leave a note with feedback every time you visit new teachers' classrooms. Let them know that there are things that they are doing well and that you are recognizing these when you are in their class.

Chat and Chew: Hold "principal's breakfasts" with just your new staff, and do so often. Have open discussions around teacher-suggested topics or new teacher concerns and questions.

Shopping 101: If the budget allows, provide a small amount of spending money for instructional supplies and classroom materials that are not available in the regular school supplies.

You Were Hired Because...: As you hold individual conferences with your new teachers, take time to share with them why they were hired. Talk about the positive characteristics that led you to hire them and what you believe are their strengths that will support the standards and expectations of the school. Explain what talents and abilities will be needed to effectively teach the children and work collaboratively with the school community.

Everybody Has a Story to Tell: Provide a time at each staff meeting for teachers to share a story about true experiences with students and their classrooms. It will confirm their work and show they are not alone in this profession.

HELPING NEW TEACHERS
RISE TO THE CHALLENGE

The challenges facing new educators today are overwhelming at first. Administrators have the opportunity to help teachers tame the standards, tackle classroom management, and teach all students as if they were their own children. As you reflect on your year as an administrator or teacher leader, take time to assess the effect you have had on new teachers' development. Do they want to come back? The skills and the knowledge level of those new teachers have grown tremendously over the year, so it is beneficial to everyone if they return to your site next year. An effective teacher retention process takes an investment of time and energy and a reorganization of priorities. The strategies and stories shared here are merely starting points and suggestions; every school has its own experiences that should be shared with beginning staff.

There is a predictable lack of predictability in the day-to-day world of teaching. As new teachers quickly discover, "perfect" teaching days are rare. Just when you think you have seen it all, there is always one more student or occurrence to change your perception of teaching, and sometimes make you think that this job is just not humanly possible.

Though the solution to the teacher retention problem cannot be found in any single process, assessing your needs and starting or supplementing a plan at your site is the beginning. The success of the process will be measured through an analysis of retention data over time, including the percentage of teachers who finish their first year and return the next year.

Every new teacher deserves support and guidance from a process that builds skills and knowledge and provides the opportunity to grow professionally. You must make the decision to focus on retaining teachers, rather than constantly recruiting them. Start small with the process, revise as needed, and celebrate success on a weekly basis. You can make a difference with new teachers. It is our responsibility at the school level to provide support in order to develop qualified and knowledgeable educators. By sharing strategies that enable new teachers to manage their classrooms, plan their instruction and assessments, and connect with their students, administrators can turn inexperienced, insecure new teachers into successful, seasoned educators who will be a credit to the school system for years to come.

References

Ainsworth, L. (2003). *"Unwrapping" the standards.* Englewood, CO: Advanced Learning Press.

Darling-Hammond, L. (1997). *Doing what matters most: Investing in quality teaching.* New York, NY: National Commission of Teaching & America's Future and Teachers College Press.

Howard, L. (2006). *Ready for anything: Supporting new teachers for success.* Englewood, CO: Advanced Learning Press.

Ingersoll, R. (2001). Teacher turnover and teacher shortages: An organizational analysis. *American Educational Research Journal, 38*(3), 499–534.

Ingersoll, R. M. (2003). *Is there really a teacher shortage? A research report co-sponsored by The Consortium for Policy Research in Education and The Center for the Study of Teaching and Policy.* Seattle, WA: University of Washington.

Kleine-Kracht, P. (1993). Indirect instructional leadership: An administrator's choice. *Education Administration Quarterly, 29*(2), 187–212.

Learning Forward. (2012). *Standards for professional learning.* Retrieved from http://learningforward.org/standards-for-professional -learning#.UZVCJlo-tqs

Robinson, V. M. J. (2006). Putting education back into educational leadership. *Leading & Managing, 12*(1), 62–75.

CONCLUSION

Making It Happen

Rachel Syrja

There is no doubt about it: the implications for educators of the Common Core State Standards are both exciting and daunting. The "fewer, clearer, higher" Common Core State Standards, anchored by the next generation assessments, will raise the bar for most states to help ensure that every student is challenged to achieve and succeed. The new assessments will measure not just what students know, but also what they can do with that knowledge. As a result, teachers will need to shift how they teach and how they assess students. By the same token, students will need to adapt to those instructional changes, but neither can be expected to do so overnight. The transition to new standards and assessments will require increased instructional capacity to support teachers in developing and expanding their repertoire of skills in anticipation of the new measures of achievement. The strategies presented in this book can help teachers begin to expand that repertoire.

The International Center for Leadership in Education finds that while education research is plentiful and comprehensive, making it possible to prove or disprove almost anything, "most of the respected research is consistent on one key school improvement issue: effective instruction really matters. No single variable has more impact than teaching" (Daggett, 2011). Despite many opinions to the contrary, there have been numerous recent research studies that have made clear that the classroom teacher is the single most influential factor in student achievement (Hattie, 2009).

HOW DO WE IDENTIFY
THE STRATEGIES
THAT WORK BEST FOR US?

In our constant effort to "cover" as much content as possible, we seldom take a moment to stop and ask if what we are doing is working. Douglas Reeves' landmark 90/90/90 research study (a look at schools with 90 percent or more of students receiving free or reduced lunch, 90 percent belonging to an ethnic minority, and 90 percent achieving or exceeding the state academic standards in reading or another subject) established that one of the best practices that schools can engage in is the constructive use of data (Reeves, 2006). Teachers at these 90/90/90 schools rely on a cyclical process of collecting and analyzing data to determine the effectiveness of the strategies they use. This reflective process allows teachers to identify the cause data, or adult actions, that yielded the results achieved. This Data Teams process can not only help educators identify the instructional practices that bring about the best results, but also help us replicate those results. We were introduced to this strategy in more than one chapter in this anthology, which is a testament to its effectiveness when implemented with fidelity. The best way to identify what works with our students is to engage in a process like Data Teams on a consistent basis. When instructional units of study based on the Common Core are anchored with well-written and aligned common formative pre- and post-assessments, teachers can determine the instructional starting point for the CCSS they are about to teach. Armed with this information, teachers can then plan lessons and select instructional strategies that help them get their students from where they currently are to where they need to be. At the end of the unit, teachers can administer the common formative post-assessment and determine the effectiveness of the lessons and strategies they utilized in the unit. These data then help the team identify what worked and also what didn't work, which will, in turn, help educators replicate our results and ensure that all students reach proficiency on the CCSS.

IMPLEMENTATION MATTERS

I have been fortunate to be in a position where I have had the opportunity to visit K–12 rural, suburban, and inner-city classrooms across the country. There are a couple of widely held opinions that I would like to challenge based upon those experiences. In my 18 years working in a suburban school district with high levels of poverty and students for whom English was a second language, I developed a very insular notion about the students I worked with. I started to believe that my students and their needs were unique, and that no teacher understood those differences better than me. I would listen suspiciously to researchers in education who would propose strategies and ideas that had worked in other districts across the country. My conclusion was always the same, and it may sound quite familiar to you: "That may have worked in that particular school or district, but our students are different, and because of those differences we can't assume that those strategies would work here." I can now say with certainty that while those instincts were partially correct, they were also partially mistaken. We know from research that the element that matters most when implementing instructional strategy or practice is degree of implementation. In fact, Doug Reeves (2010) has found in study after study that while we may assume that results increase with each incremental improvement in implementation, the research shows that the greatest gains come from deep implementation, and that there is a negligible difference between low and moderate levels of implementation (p. 36). In fact, in some cases, moderate implementation had less of an effect on achievement than no implementation at all (p. 36). So while I was correct in assuming that the differences in our student population mattered, what I know now is that what matters most is how I differentiate that strategy to fit the needs of my students.

DIFFERENTIATION MATTERS

The one thing I have witnessed in classroom after classroom, in state after state, and in rural and urban populations alike, is that good teaching strategies work everywhere and with all students. What I have also come to realize, however, is that it is the differentiation of the strategies that matters most to affecting educational outcomes. In fact, I have seen good teaching strategies fail in classrooms where the teacher has not taken into account the needs of the students and has not differentiated appropriately for that particular group of students. While the teacher may technically be using the strategy, the fact that students' needs have not been accounted for affects the degree of implementation and also impacts the efficacy of the strategy. Full implementation of any strategy requires that we take the needs of our students into account, then differentiate the strategy appropriately to meet those needs.

WHAT WE DO MATTERS

Thomas Jefferson once wrote, "Whenever you do a thing, act as if all the world were watching." As educators, we do not have the luxury to "act" as if all the world is watching, because the fact is, everyone truly *is* watching.

As educators, our "thing" is teaching. It's what we do. But we need to remember that the act of teaching should result in learning for all students. Unfortunately, that end is not always attained. In fact, as mentioned previously, we are currently faced with staggering statistics about the number of students who drop out of school every year. John Almarode, in his chapter on student engagement, stated that according to a report released by the National Center for Education Statistics (2012), approximately 8,300 students drop out of high schools every day. Disturbingly, that figure translates into approximately one student every 11 seconds. For these students, the unfortunate fact is that their investment in learning has not paid off. As a society, we cannot afford to continue to lose students at this alarming rate. We must act—and act urgently—to raise the level of engagement of our students by designing lessons that are relevant and challenging and by using effective strategies to deliver those lessons.

WHERE DO WE GO FROM HERE?

From parents to community members, policy makers to governmental officials, everyone has an opinion about how we can improve teaching and learning. We are surrounded by opinions and ideas about what works. While we are all eager to hear new ideas and learn better ways of doing things, we also need practical solutions grounded in research. The stakes are too high. Opinions, instincts, and intentions cannot guide the critical decisions we make about instruction. But this is no time for a wild goose chase. Since the inception of the standards movement in the 1990s and the accountability that accompanied the standards in the form of the No Child Left Behind legislation, we have been inundated by new initiatives, each claiming to be the solution we've been desperately searching for. However, it is precisely this eagerness to jump from one initiative to another that has oftentimes proved to be our worst enemy. Schools, and more importantly teachers, are feeling more fractured and overburdened than ever before, because the intense pressure to show results has led them on a wild goose chase for the ultimate "silver bullet," which more often than not actually turns out to be a combination of disjointed programs and initiatives. When one initiative fails to deliver, we drop it and move to the next one. There's a better way.

LET'S MAKE IT HAPPEN

Rather than buying into one more failed program or initiative, the CCSS initiative challenges us to look within ourselves for the answers. Teachers are our greatest asset, and when provided with the time and resources, amazing things can happen. The first thing we should do is stop and take inventory of everything we are currently doing. The Implementation Audit™ offered by The Leadership and Learning Center is a process that does just that. It helps us identify the degree of implementation of every current school/district initiative. This information helps schools and districts identify which initiatives are worth continuing and which need to be abandoned. Schools and districts are then freed to leverage those resources more wisely and invest where it matters most—in their human capital.

Next, we need to use multiple data points to identify the core content area(s) where our students struggle most. Additionally, we should identify the subgroup(s) that are performing the lowest. We should use the multiple data sources to help us identify the exact concepts and skills that our students are missing. Once we have this information, we can use resources such as this anthology to identify the high-impact strategies we think will help close the achievement gap for our students. Finally, we should use the Data Teams process to help us differentiate our instruction, monitor implementation of the strategies, and identify the strategies that work best with our students. While implementation of the CCSS is simultaneously exciting and daunting, we are now armed with all of the information we need to begin the process. What are we waiting for?

References

Daggett, W. R. (2011). *The Daggett system for effective instruction: Where research and best practices meet.* Rexford, NY: International Center for Leadership in Education.

Hattie, J. (2009). *Visible learning: A synthesis of over 800 meta-analyses relating to achievement.* New York, NY: Routledge.

National Center for Education Statistics. (2012). *Status dropout rates (Indicator 33-2012)*. Washington, DC: Institute of Education Sciences.

Reeves, D. (2006). *The learning leader: How to focus school improvement for better results*. Alexandria, VA: ASCD.

Reeves, D. (2010). *Transforming professional development into student results*. Alexandria, VA: ASCD.

Index

Listening, 85, 110, 154, 165, 183, 189, 220
Literacy, 61, 69, 110, 114, 148, 202, 215, 232, 233, 249
  science, 152–154, 165
  standards for, 118, 119, 147, 152, 217, 220, 227, 233
  technological, 15–16, 164
Literature, 114, 116–117, 153

Management, 59, 60, 61, 246, 249
Mathematics, 13, 50, 62, 68, 89, 94, 123–124, 128, 129, 130, 133–134, 137, 142, 150, 151, 153, 157, 166, 202, 210, 240, 246, 257
  CCSS and, 126, 143, 147, 156, 238
  knowledge/skills in, 195
  leading toward, 72–73
  learning, 125, 139, 140
  literacy and, 233
  problem solving and, 139
  questions in, 127, 128
  standards for, 149, 210, 245
Metacognition, 76, 82–85, 93, 94, 134, 219
Mistakes, learning from, 47, 126–127, 142, 143, 165
Models, 82, 86, 87, 151, 156, 159, 160
Monitoring, 44, 52, 53, 63, 73, 83, 92, 129, 171, 243, 246
  progress, 196, 198–199
Multimedia, 8, 10, 17, 118, 120, 122

National Research Council, 123, 124, 126, 150, 151, 152, 153
National Science Education Standards (National Academy of Sciences), 147, 153, 157
Next Generation Science Standards (NGSS), xvii, 44, 93, 119, 146, 147, 148, 149–152, 155, 156, 160, 164, 165, 166, 238, 240, 245, 246, 247, 251
Nicholas' cage, 130, 131

Observations, 44, 120, 141, 145, 158, 160, 247
Opinion, 103–105, 109, 110, 262
Organizations, 25, 26, 31, 104, 204–205, 240, 249
Outcomes, 5, 91, 193, 197, 198, 207, 209, 249, 260

Partnership for Assessment of Readiness for College and Careers (PARCC), 70, 76, 93, 119, 120, 121, 248
Performance, 64, 66, 67, 68, 71, 103, 120, 145, 148, 150, 162
Persuasion, 100–102, 109
Planning, 23, 30, 89, 138, 196, 239
Poster method, 134–139
Principals
  role of, 59–60, 243, 248–251
  strategies for, 251–252
Priorities, 62–63, 125, 253
Priority Standards, 64, 92, 217
Problem solving, 81, 90, 91, 125–126, 133, 146, 148, 151, 154, 155–157, 163, 201, 220
  advanced, 156
  capacity for, 138
  challenges of, 134
  daily, 127–132
  group, 137
  implementing, 138
  integrating, 155–157
  mathematics and, 139
  persevering in, 124, 131, 135
  proficiency in, 165
  research and, 153
  strategies for, 219
  structured approach to, 155
  teaching, 138
Problems, 89, 90, 131
  defining, 155, 156
  investigating, 138, 165
Professional development, 19, 26, 31, 140, 172, 200, 204–205, 232, 240, 241, 249, 250, 254
Professional learning communities (PLCs), 23, 31–34, 35, 199
Proficiency, 65, 92, 165, 173, 177, 197, 216
  language, 171, 177–183, 188, 189, 194
Progress, monitoring, 27, 29, 83, 171, 196, 198–199, 201

Questions, 47, 72, 83, 86, 87, 99, 120, 135, 140, 249
  asking, 131, 155, 156
  essential, 47, 77, 228
  mathematical, 127, 128